THE
ANTIQUE RESTORER'S
HANDBOOK

THE
ANTIQUE RESTORER'S
HANDBOOK

BY GEORGE GROTZ

A DICTIONARY OF THE CRAFTS
& MATERIALS USED IN RESTORING
ANTIQUES AND WORKS OF ART

DOUBLEDAY & COMPANY, INC., GARDEN CITY, N.Y.
1976

Library of Congress Cataloging in Publication Data

Grotz, George.
The antique restorer's handbook.

1. Antiques—Conservation and restoration—Handbooks,
manuals, etc.   I. Title.
NK1127.5.G74   745.1′028
ISBN 0-385-05302-9
Library of Congress Catalog Card Number 75-40702

For HELEN, MARIA,
and BENJAMIN

Salud, amor y dinero!

PREFACE

Restoring Antiques for Fun or Profit

Whenever you write instructions about something, you find yourself constantly saying "do this," "do that." And "Next, you must . . ." and so on.

Well, for all such authoritarian terminology, please accept this as a blanket apology. *Of course*, the mind of the antiques and art restorer should always be a clear, still pool of doubt, unclouded by any premises or precepts that may have dropped into it from time to time, so that each new job that is undertaken is a new beginning and a process of learning.

That's the fun of it!

As for the profit, take the cash and let the credit go.

GEORGE GROTZ
Provincetown, 1976

Behold, we count them happy which endure. Ye have heard of the patience of Job . . .

CONTENTS

ALABASTER

For the record, there are two kinds of alabaster. The first is the kind that was used for vases and such by the Egyptians and other ancient peoples. They found it in caves as stalactites and stalagmites. (The first is the one that hangs down; the other sticks up.) It is white, carvable, and about as hard as marble, but it hasn't been used since the great deposits of marble were found in Greece and Italy.

The second kind of alabaster, which is the one we are familiar with, was discovered in the earth in the early Middle Ages and has been mined and widely used ever since. It is mostly white, but can be yellow or red and is sometimes clouded. But its essential characteristic is that it is highly translucent—more so than any other stone. This is because it is a deposit of limestone (technically a sulphate of lime) that at some time in the earth's history was subject to enough heat to crystallize it. You could call it nature's porcelain.

So what you get when you carve alabaster is a glow and shadow of light that goes more than a half inch below the surface of the stone—only apparent, of course, if the surface is polished. Which makes alabaster a fascinating material, but it has it's faults.

It is so soft that it scratches easily—even with your fingernail if you have a hard fingernail. Also, it is slightly water soluble, so you can't make statues out of it that are to be left out in the rain. In fact, you can't even use water to clean it. You have to use mineral spirits or benzene or a dry-cleaning fluid used for clothing. And you apply these with a soft brush or cloth so as not to dull the polished surface. After cleaning, you should polish the surface with a paste furniture wax. This will both protect the surface and improve its luster, or penetration of light into the stone.

Now as to gluing broken pieces back together or patching chipped ones! You just can't. At least not without your repair being painfully obvious. The translucence defeats you completely. Just as the crack itself interrupts the flow of light, so no glue is going to make that interruption less obvious. All it can do is to keep the break from getting worse looking by keeping dirt out of it.

Of course you go ahead and glue it, using one of the two-tube epoxy glues the same way you do when mending china or porcelain. (See CERAMICS.)

As for patching, there are no translucent fillers, and probably the best thing you can do is recarve the remaining surface to make the fact that a piece is missing less obvious.

However, in the removal of stains we are luckier with alabaster because while you don't want to put water on alabaster, oxalic-acid crystals (from a paint store) can be dissolved not only in water but also in denatured alcohol. And oxalic acid (basically used for black spots caused by leaving flower pots on table tops) is also very effective on rust stains, even ink and dyes. You make a saturate solution and apply it with a pad of cloth that you keep wetting for a couple of hours. Rubber gloves are not needed unless you have a scratch on your fingers (it will sting like iodine or alcohol). But it does not burn skin or fabric or wood. It just bleaches—in spite of its scary name.

If this leaves a dull surface, the way you get back your surface shine is by burnishing it with pumice. The pumice is wetted to a thick paste and rubbed across the surface with a fingernail polisher or a block of hard felt. Finally, of course, you polish with a paste furniture wax.

AMBER

The resin that drips from fir and pine trees is best known as a base for varnish. But if it sits buried in the earth for a geological age or so, it becomes amber, hardening enough so that you can make beads and pipe stems and such out of it. But all kinds of things will soften and dissolve it: turpentine, mineral spirits, lacquer thinner, alcohol. So about the only thing you can clean it with is mild soap and water. For gluing broken pieces back together use a two-tube epoxy cement. (See CERAMICS.)

BAROMETERS

There are, of course, two kinds of barometer. One is the *stick* barometer, in which atmospheric pressure pushes a column of mercury up and down in a glass tube about thirty-four inches long. When high pressure pushes the level of the mercury up over the thirty-inch mark, you have good weather coming. When low pressure lets the level fall below twenty-nine inches rain and bad weather are on their way.

A stick barometer can consist of a straight glass tube almost filled with mercury and inverted into an open cup of mercury. Or it can be a curved tube with the mercury in the shorter arm of the tube exposed to the air. These were mostly made from 1650 to 1850, but they were hand-blown, so you can't get replacement parts. However, a glass blower can replace a broken tube if the age and the interest of the case makes the cost worthwhile.

On the other hand, the *aneroid* barometer, which came into being around 1850, can usually be "repaired" quite easily because about the only thing that can go wrong with it is that its fine, watchlike lever and gears get dirty. The lever and gears magnify the expansion and contraction of a hollow disk as the atmospheric pressure on it changes.

There are many variations on how this is done, but how yours works will be obvious after a few minutes of examination from behind, as you gently move the pointer in front a quarter inch in either direction.

Cleaning is best done by flushing on gasoline with a camel's-hair brush three-sixteenths of an inch in diameter.

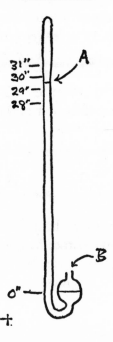

Stick barometer. Rise and fall of top level of mercury column (A) shows degree of atmospheric pressure in inches of length of column. Open end of tube (B) is where atmospheric pressure gets in.

The gasoline may be leaded or unleaded. Benzene will do as well.

And here's the secret. You apply tiny drops of watch oil with a big needle *to the bearings only.* No oil on the teeth of any gears, large or small, or on fine chains or fine springs. The point at which a rod from the disk presses against one end of a lever is considered a bearing. You can buy watch oil from your local watch repairer.

Of course, in the case of actual physical damage having

been done to the works of a barometer, a watchmaker who likes you knows where to order replacement parts—even the atmosphere-sensitive disks—and how to modify and install them. Though some watchmakers are incredibly limited and have mean little hearts, there are still those few who are delighted with such out-of-the-way projects.

BOOKS

Under this heading we cover the problems that bugs and mildew create in cloth and leather bindings. For problems that occur with the pages, see PAPER and ENGRAVINGS. For more about repairs to leather bindings, see LEATHER.

Bugs

Silverfish and book lice are the commonest bugs, and what they like best is that nice juicy glue in the bindings. Also worms will come out of the wood of your bookcase to join the feast and eat anything around.

Keeping books in a dry place will help with mildew (see page 9) but not with bugs. Once arrived, bugs don't seem to need much moisture. Witness the bugs that can live in furniture for years even in modern heated apartments. The only answer is fumigation, but be not dismayed for that is not as hard as it sounds.

All you need is a powerful antiseptic called thymol, which is made from dissolving oil of thyme (thymol) in ether or alcohol. This you get from your friendly local druggist. But he has to be really friendly because he is not likely to have it in stock and will have to order it for you the next time the salesman stops by. It comes in pint cans, and you use it in a well-ventilated place, like out-of-doors on a balmy day in May, for instance.

Then, using a soft brush, you flow, flood, soak the stuff right onto the back of the binding. You then pop the book into a tin cake box and leave the box in the sun for an hour.

If you have a lot of books to do, you can make up your own fumigation box with wire racks in it—like those in an oven—on which to lay opened books. In this case, you pour your etherized thymol in a pan in the bottom, and let the fumes work overnight. Of course, your box must be airtight to keep the fumes at saturation point.

Cloth Bindings

The most interesting cloth bindings are the colorfully illustrated ones of the second half of the Victorian era, which were stamped with a paintlike opaque ink, as in the lithography printing we find on tin cans and posters.

The surface to which these decorations were applied consists of heavily sized cloth. With minor variations, the size is a mixture of flour paste and brown animal glue with whiting (chalk), powdered colors, and dyes added. Sometimes powdered clays were also used for body and surface characteristics.

To restore chipped or worn decoration use *gouache*, a superior kind of poster color obtainable at any good art-supply store. You will be amazed at what a good job you can do because the colors were applied in solid blocks of color—no tones. Frayed edges are best touched up with regular water colors, for the *gouache* will crack and powder.

Of course, cleaning and dressing for the preservation of these bindings cannot be done with a water-based preparation. So be very careful of any spray polishes. The only things you can be sure of are paste furniture polishes and clear (not white) furniture oils. Or pure lanolin from the drugstore.

For covers that have been damaged by water, clean them first with a cleaning fluid sold for clothing or with benzene. Then try retouching them with ordinary water colors, moving up to the opaque ones if necessary, and finally wax them gently. A special dressing for these covers is manufactured and can be obtained through your friendly librarian.

Leather Bindings

Before you begin to restore a leather binding it should definitely have a thymol fumigation for bugs, as discussed on page 6. This will prevent infestation in the future. How long it will do so depends on the conditions the book is exposed to, but it will last for many years.

Most cleaning of leather bindings can be done with mild soap and water on a soft cloth. You rinse off the soap with another wet cloth. If some unclean matter still remains, you can try mineral spirits, moving on to lacquer thinner and even paint removers. The last you carefully apply just to the spot—of, say, paint—and carefully scrape off as the substance becomes soft. Clean off any residue of the paint remover with soap and water.

Now, the obvious problem with leather bindings is that they are a fibrous, porous material that dries out because the process of tanning has removed the natural oils, and not enough oil was put back in. So the just-as-obvious treatment is to reimpregnate the leather with oil.

For doing this, no less an authority than the British Museum recommends any of the following: lanolin, castor oil, sperm oil, or plain old Vaseline, which is just an easy way of buying petroleum jelly. You can get it in any supermarket.

But for the really committed, the British Museum decrees the following mixture, which you can make yourself, heating the ingredients in a double boiler, stirring with one hand while holding a fire extinguisher in your other. I list the ingredients in the order in which they go into the pan:

½ ounce beeswax (chopped for faster melting)
1 ounce mineral oil (or cedar oil or lemon oil)
7 ounces lanolin (from drugstore)
11 ounces of benzene (or less for a thicker mixture)

In England you can buy this formula premixed under the unlikely name, British Museum Leather Dressing. How's that for being straightforward?

However, when all is said and done, for a leather binding that is in really bad condition, powdery, and otherwise ready to fall apart in your hands, the best thing—as practiced by rare-book dealers—is to soak it with melted paraffin. This is the same paraffin that is sold in grocery stores for sealing the tops of jelly jars. It gives the leather more body than the dressing and will hold it together if you don't leave the book lying around in the sun. For maximum penetration, you warm the book first until it feels warm in your hands. Then you brush on the paraffin.

Mildew

The reason that mildew relates particularly to books is that it is a fungus that can grow only in damp, dark places, and books are often kept or stored in such places. In English castles that means any place, even when the books are stored in open wall bookcases.

So we turn again to the British Museum for the most knowledgeable recommendations concerning mildew. In addition to drying out your bookcase—or castle—they recommend the thymol fumigation discussed on page 6 under *Bugs*.

However, you can also destroy mildew by brushing it with powdered sulphur. For more about the many and trying afflictions to which paper is subject, see PAPER.

BOTTLES

Embossed bottles and bottles of interesting shapes date back to the Revolution, and their varieties ran wild during the 1800s. They were used for whiskey, soda pop, bitters, medicines, cleaners, flavor extracts, inks, food flavorings, oils, and so forth, in a number estimated to be over ten thousand varieties by people who prospect for them in old and sometimes historic dumps. Because they have often been buried in wastes of all kinds of chemical composition, many have acquired an opalescence that is rightly treasured. Others show signs of their contents having evaporated inside of them, which some people consider a valuable historical fact. So the cleaning of them, and the extent of cleaning, become matters of taste and discrimination.

However, if clean them you must, the solutions that will remove the various kinds of deposits on the glass are vinegar, ammonia, Clorox, and lye. In the case of lye, which is the strongest, you will want to dissolve two rounded tablespoonfuls in a pint of water. Always add the lye crystals to the water, sprinkling it in. Pouring water onto lye can give you a small but disturbing volcanic eruption with droplets of it burning holes in both your skin and your clothing. (If this does happen, neutralize immediately by pouring on vinegar.)

To get these solutions scrubbing the inside of a bottle, add sand and swirl the mixture around. If, even after this cleaning, the inside of a bottle remains dull from the chemical action on the surface of the glass, it usually can be "polished" by swirling lead shot or ball bearings around the inside. This is because glass is, technically, a cooled liquid, and its surface always remains malleable to some extent.

In fact, because of the workability of the surface of glass, minor scratches and scuff marks can also be removed by hard polishing with jeweler's rouge. For this you will want a small electric polishing and grinding machine that fits in your hand and is available in larger hardware stores.

For bringing glass to a high shine use silver polish. For stains that will react to nothing else use nitric acid in the diluted solution that is sold by drugstores.

For more information on treating glass see GLASSWARE and PAPERWEIGHTS.

BRASS

Whether or not you polish your brass furniture fittings, hardware, candlesticks, and andirons seems to depend on whether you come from the South (shiny) or New England (dull). If you have moved West, it depends on whichever you identify with.

The dullness is, of course, a patina formed by exposure to the air, and shiny brass can be kept that way by spraying it with clear lacquer. The way you make it shiny is to clean it with ammonia and water and then rub it hard with a paste-consistency mixture of vinegar and salt. Oxalic acid (saturate solution) and salt is even stronger and produces the same effect with less rubbing. Both will leave a haze on the surface that can be removed with any metal polish. (The effective ingredient in these is pumice.)

On the other hand, if you have shiny brass that you want to put a two-hundred-year-old patina on, that is easy, too. The first method is to heat the item in a kitchen oven—set at warming temperature—and then brush it with powdered graphite, which is sold in hardware stores as a substitute for lubricating oil.

For an even darker patina, you must dip the piece into, or brush it with, a solution made by dissolving 1 ounce of copper nitrate, 1 ounce of zinc sulphate, and one ounce of mercury sulphate in three cups of water, and add a quarter cup of vinegar. Soaking your piece overnight in a bowl or wetted cloths will give you the maximum result from this solution.

For further information on patinas, see BRONZE, which is the metal of which most antique statuary was made.

If a brass piece is broken, and the joint can be well cleaned and scratched, the parts can be glued with epoxy cement. (See CERAMICS.) But a better job can be done with silver solder, which can be brought from a jeweler's-supply house such as Grieger's, 900 South Arroyo Parkway, Pasadena, California 91109. Mending with silver solder is a demanding job, and for details see JEWELRY.

BRONZE

Whereas brass is an alloy of copper and zinc and is fairly soft, bronze is copper and tin and a lot harder—essentially, bronze can also have some zinc and lead in it, and in the olden days everybody had his own formula.

When unlacquered or unwaxed bronze is exposed to the air, especially damp air near the sea, it acquires a strong and lovely bluish-green patina—as opposed to the dull brown that forms on brass—which is certainly to be treasured and not removed for *any* reason. Brass, you can decide whether to shine or not, but not bronze. Only a Visigoth would clean bronze, and then only because he had a sword blade made of it (rough cast, and the edges ground sharp).

But in case some cretin *has* polished your ancient Greek, Roman, or Victorian statue, the patina can be quickly restored by cleaning it again, washing the surface with acids, and heating it in your oven at 400° F.

The simplest method is to clean the piece with soap and water, mineral spirits, and lacquer thinner, and even fine steel wool dipped in liquid soap. Use any or all of these things in any order. Just get it clean. You can even use a stiff brush and scouring powder for, regardless of what others may tell you, abrasion of the surface may dull it, but that doesn't matter. In this process of prepatination, it might even help.

Then you soak the surface using rags wetted with muriatic acid, which is widely available in hardware stores because it is used for cleaning bricks. After an overnight soak, you bake the piece in the oven for an hour.

For a faster if more nervous job, you can use hydrochloric acid (really just a stronger muriatic acid), which you get from your garage as "battery acid." If you prefer, you can use lemon juice or oxalic acid or any acid, and the reason for mentioning them all is that, depending on the make-up of the metal, proportions of copper, etc., each acid will give a slightly different color.

My favorite method, because the materials are handiest, is to scour the cleaned surface with a paste made by wetting salt with vinegar. You will notice that this leaves a strong haze on the surface, which shows how much the surface molecules have been affected. This is then baked at 400° F. to darken. For another effect you can brush it with powdered graphite (also from your hardware store) before baking at 400° F. There are no rules, and there is no way of telling the shade or color you will get, because of the varying content of the different metals.

The color of these artificially created patinas will often change in a few days after treatment—although, once this has happened, they will remain stable.

Actually, these methods of patination also apply to brass and copper—as well as to any of the "soft" metals such as lead, silver, gold, German silver, pewter—except that the full-strength hydrochloric (battery) acid should be used only on bronze.

As for repairing bronze, it isn't often that anything of bronze breaks, but an arm of a statuette or sword blade can be tacked back together with epoxy glue or it can be silver soldered (see BRASS and JEWELRY). But in neither case is the original strength anywhere nearly restored.

However, I do have the happy news that repairs or chipped patinas can be perfectly camouflaged. First, any little spurs sticking out from the repair are filed off. These occur because sometimes the edges of the break are bent at the time the metal is broken, and the softer the metal, the more likely this is to happen.

Then any indentations at the repair can be filled in with one of the epoxy glues filled with powdered metal—because it is less runny—and when the glue is hard it can be filed down level with the surface.

The area can now be touched up, so that it is undetectable to the human eye, with flat, opaque water colors known as *gouache*, obtainable from a good art-supply store. I use Winsor and Newton's Designer's Gouache, which comes in little tubes. The basic colors you will need are greens and browns: olive green, viridian green, burnt umber, raw umber. And for a bluish cast, add cerulean blue and lemon yellow.

A perfect color match can be mixed with these colors. It will dry dull, but if you want a little more luster, just rub the surface with your finger. For a little more shine, spray with dull clear lacquer. For further increase in shine, polish it with wax. Thus you have complete control not only of the color but also of the degree of shine or luster. (See also BRASS and COPPER and the other sections on various metals.)

BRONZE POWDER DECORATION

The Chinese were the first to use powdered metal to decorate things, and they used powdered gold. That is where the English got the idea for using powdered bronze back in the early 1800s to decorate tinware.

At first the powder was applied freehand with brushes, but for mass-production purposes, the English soon started using stencils. They not only sold the powder in England but also exported it to all the colonies. Between wars with them, of course.

The practice naturally spread to the United States, and by the 1830s the Hitchcock brothers were running wild with it, distributing their decorated chairs by peddlers all over the Northeast. And it is these chairs and the tinware of the same period that we are concerned with—from minor touch-ups to complete redecorations, for they were usually very little protected from wear by any covering coat.

This was because the surface on which the design was stenciled was a kind of shellac with black pigment in it, and brushing a protective coat over it would have lifted the powder off the surface of the undercoat. This is why any supposedly original decoration that isn't in very bad shape has to be looked upon with the most profound suspicion. It had to wear off if the object was used at all.

Also, the craft isn't all that difficult, and anybody can do it today just as it was done originally. So what I am saying is that a great deal of this kind of decoration that you see is fake. I'd say at least half of the pieces that have passed in the open market are fakes. And if you think that is a hysterical claim, I want to tell you that years ago I knew an old man in Connecticut who admitted to me that in his lifetime he had sold over six hundred Hitchcock chairs that he had redecorated and sold as having the original decoration— slightly distressed, of course. And signed on the back, too.

And I believed him, because that is only an average of two chairs a month over thirty years, and I saw twenty of them in various stages of decoration still in his shop. He had a separate little barn where he kept all his supplies and what he called his "original" stencils, which were simply exact copies that he had made of original stencilwork that he had found in pretty good condition.

So let's describe the whole process from the wood up, as this successful old crook taught it to me those many good years ago.

First the wood is sealed with three coats of shellac, each of which is sanded smooth with very fine sandpaper or the longer-lasting garnet paper. Onto these you brush two coats of a slightly thinned-down, flat, black oil-based paint. That's the kind of paint that thins with mineral spirits or turpentine. He used turpentine because that's all they had in those days, but no difference.

Do not sand the flat black paint, but after it is thoroughly dry, give it a coating of shellac. This will give you a black with a shade and luster just like the original, which was shellac with black pigment in it. This is why you can get the same effect by dissolving thick old phonograph records in denatured alcohol and painting the resulting fluid on the wood without any covering of shellac. Of course, it takes an awfully long time for the records to dissolve, even broken up in little pieces, but I just thought you might be interested.

Now let me add that in all these coatings absolute cleanness of liquids and brushes is required. Use little fresh cans of paint and shellac, and soft-haired brushes that are new or have never been allowed to dry out. The brushes for the paint must be stored suspended in cans of turpentine. The brushes for the shellac, if they are to be used again, should be stored suspended in denatured alcohol, which is hard to do because alcohol evaporates so fast. If you insist on cheating on me, be sure to wash all brushes in five or six rinses of lacquer thinner—the only really effective brush cleaner there is.

Next, the thoroughly dried surface of shellac to be stenciled on is coated with a very *thin* coat of spar varnish, which is a very *slow*-drying varnish. It is thinned by adding a tablespoonful of turpentine or mineral spirits to about two thirds of a cup of the varnish. And, of course, *fresh* varnish (which is the only clean varnish) and *clean* brushes.

This coat of spar varnish is now allowed to dry on a day of average humidity for four hours. On a dry day, for three hours. And on a damp or humid day, forget it. Don't do it that day. Anyway, it is onto this tacky varnish that you are going to put your bronze powders through the holes in your stencils.

So now about the stencils. These can be bought in arts and crafts stores, or you can make your own to duplicate something you have on hand—such as a badly worn design that you want to replace. The method is to trace the design on tracing paper and transfer this to stencil paper with carbon paper. Perfect your lines on the stencil paper with a sharp pencil, and then cut your stencil out with an Exacto knife. But don't think you can go fast. Budget a lot of your precious time for this—like a weekend—or you will get a messy, useless job.

The stencil will stick to the varnish onto which you press it —pretty firmly at the edges—and you are now ready to apply the bronzing powders.

These powders are available in a great many colors, and the ones commonly used are readily available. In addition, they can be mixed the same way oil paints are mixed on a palette. Start with a plate of glass about ten by twelve inches, and pour out about a quarter teaspoonful of each color in little mounds about three inches apart. The mixing you want to do is then done with a camel's-hair water-color brush.

To apply the powder to the tacky varnish use little pads or cotton-filled balls of silk-velvet—if you want to be traditional. But any velvet will do if you make sure on some practice surface—also coated with your tacky varnish—that it won't lose any hairs. And even if you are experienced at this process, you *will* have such a surface prepared at the same time as your real work surface to test if the tackiness of the varnish is right for receiving the powder. So you dip your velvet applicator in the powder and lightly tap it on the tacky varnish left exposed by your stencil—after having tried it out on your practice surface first, of course.

It works beautifully.

When you have finished blow off any excess bronze powder. Or dust it off with a large camel's-hair brush if you can afford one, and carefully lift the stencil while saying a prayer that no bronze powder has gotten under its edges. If it has, you might be able to scratch it off with your Exacto knife, but I doubt it. Best to wash everything off with mineral spirits, and start again with a new coating of the spar varnish.

Now, I didn't want to interrupt the narration so there are two footnotes to be added to this. The first is that shellac cannot be used in humid weather because the alcohol in it will pick up molecules of the water in the air and cause a white film on the surface, which is called a "blush." This can sometimes be rubbed off with steel wool, but not always, and you are removing shellac in the process. If this happens, it is best to wait for a dry day and apply another coat of shellac, which will make the blush disappear.

The other thing is that if you are not some kind of old-fashioned purist, you can simplify matters a great deal by using spray cans of flat black paint or lacquer and, instead of shellac, a spray can of dull or matte clear lacquer. This eliminates all the hassle of the brushes and the paint and shellac having to be absolutely clean and fresh, and I don't think anybody can tell the difference.

Now, in the case of a Hitchcock chair, which this is mostly about, the penultimate step is to sign your work across the back of the seat. This is not done with a stencil, as is the case with the modern reproductions of these chairs, but with a fine camel's-hair brush of the best quality—for springiness of the hairs. And the paint used is artist's oil colors thinned with poppy oil or other drying medium sold in an art-supply store. The color of the paint should be yellow ocher darkened with a little raw umber—which is a sort of gold effect that kind of matches the color of the bronze powder most commonly used. To match this perfectly with any of the bronze powder colors, you'll have to get hold of a chair with the original decoration and a "signature" to copy—though the colors the original factory put out varied from time to time, you are really pretty safe with any approximation.

Now the ultimate step, which is called distressing. You do this by rubbing your work where it would have been naturally worn down with a rough cloth such as fine-weave burlap or fine steel wool. Just be careful with the steel wool because it cuts pretty fast.

That's the whole process. As for touching up, it doesn't work very well because of the delicateness of the shades of worn-off powder. But chip-offs can be touched up, and it ill-behooves me to tell you not to try. The approach to this is to mix the powders with varnish and brush them on thinly, sometimes wiping or smudging them off rather gently with your finger.

CAST IRON

Of course, some really ancient things were made out of iron—mostly knives and tools—but iron was so hard to work that its heyday for use in artistic and ornamental things didn't arrive until the Industrial Revolution, when people first put their minds to using it to make machinery.

Once they had learned to melt iron and cast it in molds made of a fine, wet sand contained in wooden boxes, they soon had all kinds of things made out of it. About the earliest was Franklin's fine little stove. Then came many other stoves, and pots, fences, garden ornaments, match holders, toys, and so on.

The virtue of cast iron is its great strength. The trouble with it is its brittleness, which comes from the fact that it is virtually pure iron, which cools off with a crystalline structure. But all cast iron isn't alike because if it is cooled off slowly—over a matter of days—it will be less brittle.

Only the small pieces, such as toys, can be mended with epoxy glue since the bigger things were made of iron in the first place because they had to take a lot of stress. Or heat. And epoxy is the *best* method of repairing small things; the other methods of welding or brazing make a big mess at the break. But an epoxy mend is easily made invisible with matching paints. (For more on this, see BRONZE.)

Breaks in things like fences and stoves can be done by your local welder. He has two methods—welding and brazing. In welding he uses steel, and this is the strongest. But this is done at such a high temperature that there is danger of melting the cast iron. His preferred method is brazing, which is welding with a brass rod at a lower temperature. This should be done on both sides of the crack if possible. Then the outside of the mend, which will rise above the surface, can be brought down flush with a grinding wheel on a quarter-inch drill or a file and, finally, garnet paper. Sometimes it is possible just to braze the inside—as in the case of the leg of a stove—and this will save a lot of grinding.

Concealment of the break on larger pieces is easily done with a spray can of flat black paint. Blackening such pieces this way is standard practice.

CERAMICS

With ceramics we're mostly talking about chinaware, but the word "ceramics" covers the whole field of things made out of baked clays that have fused into an undissolvable solid. From ancient times until yesterday.

To avoid confusion from the start, it should be understood that this includes porcelain, which is baked from a special clay called kaolin. Kaolin fuses to a mildly translucent state—thin porcelain letting through about as much light as milk glass, for instance.

Porcelain was first discovered by the Chinese of the Ming dynasty, which began in the year 1368. It was the original "China-ware" brought back from the Orient by early European explorers.

The English immediately became very enthusiastic about this stuff and set up many factories to produce "China-ware." But they didn't know about the kaolin, and so the great English (and European) chinaware up to the 1700s is opaque. In other words, the Chinese kept their secret for some four hundred years—although at one point, various English factories were putting ground glass into their clay to get a pretty good imitation.

The names and histories of these processes and the various chinawares have had many books written about them for collectors, and our only concern here is their repair and the concealment of such repairs. They are all repaired the same way, although there has been a revolution in the methods during the last fifteen years. This was caused, of course, by the invention of the epoxy glues. While these were resisted for a while by the kind of old fogies who usually work in the back rooms of museums, believe me when I tell you that they are now totally accepted.

But the old way—holding the broken pieces together with tiny brass clamps made of pieces of brass wire—is so interesting to look at and such an example of the craftsmanship of its times, that I think it should be preserved. Also, pieces repaired this way should not be taken apart and repaired the new "invisible" way. I put the word "invisible" in quotes because this method is used so much, not because the repairs aren't truly invisible (except with porcelain when it is held up to the light).

In the old method the first step was to drill two holes opposite each other about a quarter inch from the break. In some cases these went all the way through. In others, such as a thick plate, they were drilled from the bottom and went only halfway into the material. You will have to admit this is touchy work indeed.

A piece of brass wire of suitable length was then cut and bent with tweezers into the shape of a staple with short points—to fit into the holes. Assuming exactly the right size and shape of staple were used, the points would snap into the holes and hold the two pieces together.

Now, while that may not sound very secure to you, we are talking about brass wire up to an eighth of an inch in diameter, and pieces so repaired were intended only for being put on display, without glue or any attempt to conceal the crack. However, I have seen some heavy farmhouse china repaired this way and in daily use. Amazing! On the other hand, it is *common* to find pieces of china that have been repaired with epoxy in regular use, especially pieces that have no value as antiques, for they will stand up even in very hot water. I have several coffee cups so mended that we have been using without thinking about them for three or four years.

Let us discuss this new craft, first in general and then under a number of subheads relating to different kinds of damage.

Invisible China Repair

There is an old belief that if you want to teach somebody something, the best way to do it is first to tell them what you are going to tell them, then tell them, and finally tell them what you told them. Well, I don't want to go that far, but I do think it will be helpful to make a general survey of the process first, and then take it step-by-step and deal with problems separately.

There are two hearts to the matter.

The first is that the epoxy glues (not the five-minute variety, but the twenty-four-hour-setting ones) will make a mend in any ceramic that is harder than the material itself. If you purposely rebreak your repair, it will break on one side or the other of the mend. Also, the glue is colorless (except for a couple of amber brands that you don't buy) and wipes off perfectly with denatured alcohol or even rubbing alcohol.

The second heart of the matter is not quite so nifty because it is a very delicate craft to learn. This is the use of an airbrush, which is a very fine paint sprayer, operated by a

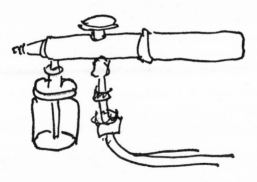

Hand-held airbrush.

small can of compressed air. The secret of this device is that a stroke of its spray over the repaired break leaves an extremely delicate feathered edge. For some reason this really fools the human eye—even if your paint is a shade different from the surface. Of course, we're not going to use paint a shade different anyway, are we? Are we? Well, maybe you are, but I'm not. I just brought it up to impress you with how remarkable this feathered-edge phenomenon is.

The reason is that a *brush* stroke of even exactly matched paint will stick out on china like a sore thumb because it is resting on the colorless glaze—which is *actually* a thin film of glass on the surface of the baked clay. As a result, it casts a sharp shadow—not a fuzzy one—which is completely visible as a narrow black line.

Of course, you can make a great many repairs without using an airbrush to cover them up because on darker pottery pieces the lines are hardly visible after an epoxy mend. Even in the case of white china, the mend line can be 75 per cent obscured by wiping some powdered chalk along the crack while the glue is still wet. The chalk can even be tinted with other powdered colors.

Before I leave the generalities of the craft of invisible china repair, I must mention that the epoxy glue can also be diluted quite thin with denatured alcohol to make a glaze for touching up areas that are dull or to brush over some decoration that we have had to paint on or touch up at a break. You don't have to use an airbrush for this; a camel's-hair brush will do because the epoxy naturally casts no shadow at a brushed-out edge.

Finally, replacing missing pieces—say, a plate or a missing handle or spout—is done by working chalk powder into the epoxy mixture until it becomes a putty, which can be sculpted after it has hardened. Also, it can be cast or pushed into a mold. It is a far stronger and better-adhering substance than plaster of Paris, although it must be said that plaster of Paris made incredibly tight fits in replacing, say, a piece broken out of the edge of a plate, because it has the strange quality of expanding ever so slightly as it sets. And what other white paste can make that claim?

Now let us go through the process step by step, these steps being:

Cleaning	Kits
Gluing	Airbrushing
Filling Chips	Decorating
Replacing Parts	Glazing

Followed by some further explanatory notes about:

Clay	Parian
Earthenware	Bisque (Biscuit)
Porcelain	Faïence
Soft Porcelain	Majolica
Bone China	Delft

Cleaning

Articles that have been freshly cracked or ones that have been kept in a box wrapped up in tissue paper should only be blown on to avoid further damage. What we are talking about are open cracks that have sucked in soil and stains, and pieces that previously have been mended with glue that has gotten dirty or changed color.

The first step in all cases is to put the piece in plain water and let it soak for twenty-four hours. Water is a great softener, and if there is any porosity to the material, the water will fill it up and prevent the occasional tragedy of some cleaning solvent pushing the dirt further in.

For a crack not previously repaired, wipe the piece clean and let the crack dry out for an hour at room temperature. Soap and detergents won't help, but there are several bleaching methods you can try.

The first and oldest of these is lemon juice or vinegar and hot sunshine. You leave the plate on a sunny window sill and apply the lemon juice and vinegar as often as you can remember to do it for a week. It works, but a little slowly.

For those of us in a hurry, the best thing to try first is to soak the crack a few minutes with straight ammonia (*non-sudsing*). Wipe the surface dry and immediately apply Clorox, working it into the crack as well as you can.

The next method to try is ammonia, followed by regular drugstore hydrogen peroxide. This is the same process as is used for bleaching hair, except that you use the ammonia full strength.

Finally, try soaking the piece with a saturate solution of oxalic acid, followed by working Clorox into the crack.

Roughly speaking, these methods work only about half the time, but that leaves them worth trying. And I assume it is obvious that your crack should be allowed to dry for an hour or so between trying the various methods. Also, no stronger acids or cleaning agents should be used, because of the danger of their setting off a degenerating chemical reaction in the clay under the glaze.

When the problem is a piece that has been previously glued—whether it is intact or in pieces—again the twenty-four-hour water soak comes first. If the glue used was an old-fashioned hide or fish glue, it will either soften or, more likely, dissolve and wash away.

In an old piece of any value the most likely glue to have been used will be shellac, the same kind we use today. Water will soften it only a little. To dissolve it, we have only to soak the piece in denatured alcohol. If the piece is too large to immerse easily, we soak it with cloth pads kept moist by repeated applications of alcohol, brushing at it between soakings with a soft brush.

I suppose that I should mention here that breathing the fumes of denatured alcohol will first give you a headache, then cause you to pass out, and finally, in an unventilated room, kill you.

That is why some people use lacquer thinner for this job. It will also dissolve the shellac and doesn't give you a headache. On the other hand, in an unventilated room, it will also cause you to pass out and eventually kill you. But without the headache!

Whatever the glue used, it should not be picked off with the corner of a single-edge razor blade or a pin, for no matter how careful you think you can be, you will surely chip away some glaze at the edges of the break. So, if you don't have the patience to dissolve and brush away the glue with a camel's-hair brush, do something else in your spare time. Maybe furniture refinishing would be better for you. Repairing china is for the kind of people who like to wear close-up magnifying glasses, even a jeweler's glass, and work slowly and painstakingly, thinking each step over before they do it.

Gluing

There are two secrets to gluing. The first is to have a dress rehearsal of the whole job. This establishes that you have all your materials within reach and determines exactly how you are going to hold your glued pieces together while the epoxy glue is setting. This can get to be a complicated matter when a piece is broken into more than two parts.

The second secret is to apply so small an amount of glue that the pieces aren't displaced by the bulk of it. This is because you cannot count on squeezing it out. In the first place, epoxy just doesn't squeeze out that easily. It is too thick and not runny enough. In the second place, pushing two or more pieces together hard is surely going to make them slip and grind their edges. This will make the mend line worse than it was in the first place and probably get a tiny pebble of the glaze into the glue between your pieces so that they won't close tightly—until you wash the glue off and start all over again.

The way you apply the glue is with the narrow end of a toothpick in a thin strip down the middle of the break surface. The strip must be thin enough so that it doesn't reach the glaze at the edges. Being nearsighted or wearing magnifying glasses will help. Now you tap the glue down with your fingertip, wiping your finger as it picks up glue on a piece of lintless cloth—such as a piece of sheet or pillow case that has been washed so often that it has begun to tear and has been retired for purposes such as this. You keep tapping until you can't feel any glue and very light tapping doesn't bring up any glue anymore, but the surface still glistens a little. Only then do you fit the pieces together and (with the exception of a crack that runs only part way across a dish) exert pressure in some way as the glue sets—which is where the rehearsal comes in.

Nobody is perfect, and it may be that although you can feel with your fingertips that you have a perfect fit, some glue will exude from the crack. In this event, you have two options. The first is to wipe the excess off with a pad of cloth wet-damp with denatured alcohol. Or you can let it sit for four hours—when it has set but not fully hardened—and slice it off with a thin double-edged razor.

Using a razor this way is not doing it the hard way for the fun of it. The point is that in some cases, maybe most, tiny pieces of glaze have broken off at the edge of the break. If you slice your glue off with a razor, you will leave glue in those minute holes that you would otherwise have to fill this very way anyhow.

Of course, this brings up the possibility of using enough glue so that some is sure to be exuded under pressure, assuring that you will be able to slice it off. Well, that is fine if you can get away with it—that is to say, if you don't displace the pieces or grind them together in pressing out the glue. It gets down to a matter of "feel"—your particular "feel" in performing this operation. To establish this feel, the obvious thing to do is to practice on junk pieces even if you have to smash a few old plates.

Now let us consider individually the gluing and clamping in the following basic problems:

1. Gluing a crack part way through a plate or vase.
2. Gluing and clamping a plate or vase broken into two parts.
3. Gluing and clamping *or supporting* a plate or vase broken into three or more parts.
4. Gluing on a spout or handle that has been broken off. (Replacing lost ones comes up later in this chapter.)

Gluing an open crack is an exception to the rule of clamping while the epoxy sets because if you did, the crack would eventually open. Even epoxy isn't immune to the kind of constant force that causes such a crack, even though the crack might open next to the join. In this case, let the epoxy fill the crack, though actually you will use an epoxy mix that has been filled with a white powder tinted to match the color of the plate. (You fill the epoxy until it becomes a soft putty.) In this instance, you unquestionably do use enough putty so that some rises above the surface of the plate; just trim it off before it hardens with a thin double-edged razor, which bends to conform to the surface of the plate on either side of the crack.

The making and coloring of an epoxy putty is explained under *Filling Chips* (page 33), but let us return to gluing with our second situation—a plate that has been broken into two pieces.

First, the epoxy mixture is applied and tapped off as described at the beginning of this section. Then you carefully join your pieces and press them firmly together. Now stick the plate on edge into a box containing balls of waxy clay or Mortite so that the top piece is exactly above the bottom piece and gravity will be pulling the top piece down for you. The clay or Mortite will hold the plate vertical.

I am aware that most people will want to exert even more pressure by using rubber bands or stickum tape. Their reasoning is that if some pressure is good, more pressure must be better. Not so, say I and those whom I have watched do this thing. A tight fit is a tight fit, and when the pull can be made straight down, gravity is good enough. So we save our tape for a plate that is broken in several pieces and, of course for round bowls and vases where there is a danger of slippage occurring before the epoxy has set.

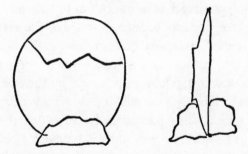

Plate held vertical by balls of Mortite while epoxy sets.

Now for that situation where a plate, bowl, or vase has been broken into three or four or more pieces. Each situation is unique, and here is where we get deep into dress rehearsal. What we are going to rehearse is our method of holding the piece together with tape and/or propping and pushing it together with modeling clay and/or balls of Mortite, a great substance for this purpose. (It is sold in hardware stores for sealing window frames in cold weather.)

Because of the slippage that is likely to occur, a piece that has been broken into more than four pieces unfortunately cannot be glued back together in one operation. But given a cup or bowl that has been broken into only four pieces, what you want to figure out by rehearsal is a way to hold all the pieces snugly together. And there are two ways.

The first is to pull the pieces together with pieces of masking tape. The second way is to push the pieces together with balls of clay or Mortite. The balls are fine around the bottom. For breaks up the side, you cut a piece of quarter-inch doweling to the appropriate length and push a ball of Mortite about an inch in diameter on each end. With these you prop up the sides from the surface the piece is standing on, or you

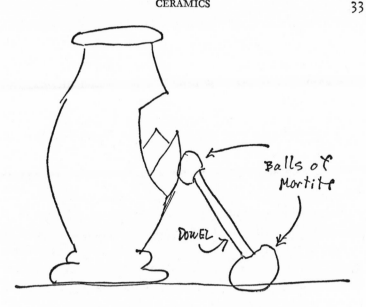

*Method of propping pieces of chinaware while
epoxy is setting.*

push them in horizontally from stacks or bricks or other
heavy objects placed in appropriate spots around the piece.

If a vase, say, is broken in twenty pieces, you have to follow
the same procedure, working up from the bottom with two or
three pieces at a time, letting them dry for twenty-four hours
before proceeding with the next few.

To reattach spouts and handles, you can use any of these
methods. But rehearse—always rehearse.

Filling Chips

Here we come to the making of a filler paste or putty for
filling edge chips and, further on, for replacing missing pieces
and even making new spouts and handles. This is done on a

glass palette measuring about ten by fourteen inches; a palette knife with a flexible end is the best tool for mixing.

What we are going to mix, of course, is our epoxy two-tube glue with a powdered clay called kaolin, which just happens to be the same clay used in the making of real porcelain. It is sold in drugstores in little boxes and tins because it is a long-time basic medicine for treating diarrhea. You can also use whiting, which is powdered chalk that you buy in boxes at paint and hardware stores, but the kaolin builds up a thicker paste a lot faster and more easily.

To tint this paste you use an ordinary set of water colors of the kind that come in little tubes. Such tubes can also be bought separately, which is useful, because you will be particularly interested in the so-called "earth colors," which do not come in most sets. These are raw umber, burnt umber, raw sienna, burnt sienna, and yellow ocher. Also ivory black and Paine's gray. Plus white, red, yellow, blue, green.

On your palette you mix a brush touch of color with a little Chinese white (also a water color) to see the tint you will get. You then mix the desired color or mixture of colors into your epoxy paste—with which you carefully fill in the chipped-out area, using enough so that the paste rises slightly above the surrounding surface.

When this has set—in about three hours—you trim it with your thin, flexible double-edged razor blade. As the setting time will vary with the degree of heat, you determine the time the paste is ready for easy slicing by testing the blob of it that remains on your palette after an hour has gone by.

When the paste has hardened—in twenty-four hours—it can also be sanded, ground, or filed. But all these are very difficult procedures because it is almost impossible not to grind on (and dull) the glaze surrounding your patch; this is why you want to do as much of the work as possible with the razor blade. But you will probably have to do a little sanding with very fine emery paper, which will leave your patch dull. You cure this by brushing it with freshly mixed clear epoxy thinned with a little alcohol—about one drop of alcohol to four drops of the mixed epoxy.

Replacing Parts

It gets harder to replace missing pieces because as you work more kaolin into the epoxy to get it to a putty consistency, you are not likely to end up with the exact tint you wanted. However, forge ahead, and we will solve the color-match problem in a minute.

In the case of a piece missing from a plate after all the other pieces have been glued together, the simple trick is to cover the hole on the face side of the plate with a piece of gummed paper of the kind used for sealing boxes. Wet the back of the paper first to soften it. Then wet the glued side and paste it down over the hole. As it dries, it will tighten and conform to the surface of the plate. Now turn the plate bottom side up. With a fine-pointed brush wet the exposed edges with clear epoxy. Then take a flattened piece of putty trimmed with a razor to approximately the size of the hole and squeeze it in between your thumb and forefinger. Using a palette knife, and more or less putty or paste as needed, finally smooth the bottom side of your patch to conform with the surrounding surface. Later this can be trimmed and sanded down and reglazed.

After twenty-four hours of drying, the paper tape on the face of the plate can be moistened and rubbed off with your finger if it doesn't just peel off. The patch can then be built up with more putty, if necessary. Then it can be sanded and glazed with clear epoxy as the back was. It is a slow process—for patient people only.

If the color is a bad match, you can mix up a thin paste of kaolin-filled epoxy tinted correctly this time, and brush it over the patch, smudging it at the edges onto the surrounding glaze with your fingertip. A really good job can be done this way, but if it still does not suit you, you will have to use an airbrush, which we will be getting to next.

As to replacing handles and spouts, these are molded with the putty and pressed onto the break places, which have been moistened with clear epoxy.

In the case of delicate cup handles, you will have to build them up around a piece of iron wire, molding and grinding them to shape before applying them. Difficult pieces will involve adding more putty and grinding it down again. This, of course, is the technique also used for replacing pieces broken off statuettes.

For such complicated sculpturing you will need a small, hand-held grinder that you can find in large hardware stores and hobby shops. It is called a Dremel Moto-Tool.

Kits

Now, before moving along to airbrushing, I want to mention that a kit is available that will handle everything we have done up to this point, using similar materials. And there are also sets of epoxy-type paints that can be used for replacing decorations or tinting epoxy putties and pastes.

The first is called Master Mending Kit for China and Glass. It includes glue, putty, six colors, and glaze—and you also get instructions tailored to these products. It's a good starter kit and at this writing is selling for $14.95. You can

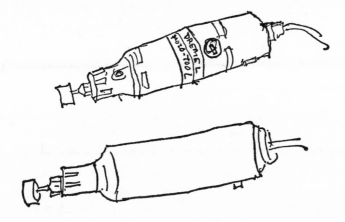

Hand-held grinder, with chuck that will also hold sanding disks, brushes, drills, etc.

send for a catalogue sheet describing it or order it from Atlas Minerals & Chemicals, Farmington Road, Mertztown, Pennsylvania 19539.

The other kit, called Ceramit, consists of a large bottle of "hardener," which you mix with the small bottles of "color." This material hardens to a ceramiclike surface when it is baked for one hour at 200° F. This is less than boiling heat and will not injure any chinaware I have ever heard about. But to avoid sudden expansion shock, you should put any piece to be so baked in a cold oven to start, and allow it to heat slowly. This is probably not necessary, but it is a reasonable precaution to take.

Ceramit is distributed through arts and crafts and hobby shops. The basic kit contains fourteen colors, plus clear and the hardener. The opaque colors are red, orange, yellow, jadegreen, turquoise, black, and white. The transparent colors are red, orange, yellow, green, reddish brown, bluish brown, blue, and clear. The kit sells for around $25, while a larger kit with

forty colors goes for around $65. Ceramit kits can also be or-
dered by mail from Grieger's, 900 South Arroyo Parkway,
Pasadena, California 91109.

Airbrushing

Concealing repairs with the fine spray that comes out of an
airbrush is not really hard to do once you have read the instructions and practiced for an hour. The main problem is
whether you want to commit yourself to the expense. The
tool itself will cost you from fifty to one hundred dollars. And
then you need an air tank for another forty dollars and a pressure regulator so that the pressure coming out of the tank can
be kept constant—for another thirty-five dollars. So the
cheapest you can get away with is a hundred and twenty-five
dollars.

What you get is a tool that will spray a fine line of paint
from a sixteenth to a quarter of an inch wide with perfectly
evenly shaded edges. When the paint matches the color of
the surface, it is undetectable to the human eye.

Any paint or lacquer can be used in this device after it has
been thinned down to the consistency of milk, but the best
thing to use is artist's oil colors of the best quality. For instance, those made by Winsor and Newton. A set will cost
you around twenty dollars, and you will want to fill it out
with umbers, siennas, and ochers as these are easier to tint
your basic white with—rather than mixing browns from
scratch with the primary colors.

To get good drying, you should mix these oil colors with
poppy oil and then thin them to the proper consistency with
turpentine; both are available at your art-supply store.

Successful color mixing is a matter of patience. You will
soon find that there are an infinite number of shades and tints

of white. Start mixing your color on a palette of glass, and when you get close, move a glob of paint over onto the piece itself to refine it further. Then remove it and thin it to spraying consistency in the cup of your airbrush. As I said in the beginning, you will be surprised how well this works to deceive the eye, even if an absolutely perfect color match has evaded you. (If you are even slightly color blind, your efforts are doomed to failure.)

Decorating

For designs that must be retouched or replaced, you will use the same oil paints mixed with poppy oil—not linseed oil, which is a very slow drier. Some reds, for instance, actually take months to dry fully when mixed with plain linseed oil.

For decorating, use the most expensive fine-pointed brushes you can buy. These are sable as opposed to camel's hair, and because they do not lose their springiness they are worth every exorbitant cent for fine work like this.

Gilded edges can be touched up with waxes containing golden shades of bronze powder, which are sold under the names of Rub & Buff and Treasure Jewels in hobby shops and art-supply stores. If you put a glaze over them, they will do very well.

Or you can apply gold leaf (see GOLD LEAFING.)

Glazing

Often a patch, a touch-up, or redecoration will have less gloss to it than the surrounding surface. Or you may just have dulled the surface around a patch with emery paper.

This can be touched up by spraying clear lacquer with your airbrush, but if you haven't gone into the airbrush scene, the easiest thing to do is to spray the whole object with a coat of clear gloss lacquer from a spray can.

But lacquer can be employed only when the piece isn't to be used. It will chip off and won't stand up under washing. A better way to restore a glaze is to use a wide camel's-hair brush (three-quarter inch) to brush on a coating of epoxy glue well-thinned with denatured alcohol. Start with a mixture of about half as much alcohol as glue and add more if necessary to get a nice flow.

Various and Sundry

Herewith some definitions and background information that may be useful in your understanding of the kind of pieces that come up for restoration.

CLAY – The basis for all ceramics is clay, which is made up of exceedingly fine particles of weathered rock. The particles are washed down rivers and there form sedimentary deposits. Clay is, therefore, found at the bottoms of mountains all over the world. When man was still living in caves he found this stuff, shaped it into bowls, and baked them over his fires. He somehow had stumbled onto the fact that heat fused the clay particles back into a new equivalent of stone.

Some of these clays bake light and porous, while others are very hard. If they contain metal oxides, they bake in different colors.

EARTHENWARE – There is sometimes a little confusion about this word. In exact English usage it means anything made by baking clay. But it just didn't sound fancy enough for delicate china and porcelain to some people, and around 1850 the word ceramics came into the English language to mean, more specifically, "artistic" things made out of clay; in popular usage the word "earthenware" has been demoted to mean the equivalent of pottery. Pottery being useful, things made out of clay were to be used—as opposed to things that are just to be looked at.

SLIP – Slip is like an opaque glaze. It is a wash of hard clay brushed on a pot made of porous clay that is then rebaked. The purpose is to make the piece waterproof. Designs are often scratched into the slip just before it is popped into the oven. If they are artistic scratchings, you have a piece of pottery that is a little like a piece of ceramics.

GLAZE – Glaze is slip made of powdered glass, which fuses in a reheating to give to the dullness of even fine baked clay a glossy and very hard surface. Starting at the bottom and working up, this is the process used in making redware, glazed terra cotta, stoneware, ironware, Bennington jugs, fine English china, and all the way up to delft and faïence. The last two have a white-glass glaze.

PORCELAIN – As I have noted at the beginning of this section, porcelain is baked from a clay called kaolin, whose elements are so similar to those of glass that it comes out of the oven fused to a translucent state.

SOFT PORCELAIN – Soft porcelain is the technical term for the imitation porcelain made in Europe up to the early 1800s, when deposits of kaolin were found there and put to use. This "soft" porcelain was made of any fine white clay loaded with ground glass, which gave varying degrees of translucence, but the surface came out dull, and it then had to be glazed in a second baking.

Soft porcelain is sometimes so hard to distinguish from the real thing that the only true test is to file a notch in the bottom with a triangular file. This will reveal if the piece is glassy all the way through or is just a fine cement covered with a glass coating.

Also, surface cracks appear only on the soft porcelain—never on the real thing. And sometimes the scuffed bottom of a soft-porcelain piece will suck in a drop of stain or ink, enough to color the surface and not wipe off—as it will from porcelain.

BONE CHINA – Naturally the factories that were trying to imitate porcelain tried many formulas, and in England one of these formulas turned out to be so much better than the rest that it was not given up even when the secret of true porcelain was discovered. This was, of course, bone china, which gets its translucence from the addition of bone ash and soapstone to the clay. As the elements do partially fuse in baking, it is halfway to being porcelain, but because it does have to be glazed to get a glossy surface it is still classified as a soft porcelain.

Since bone china is even whiter and lighter than true porcelain, there are those who think it is still better. But generally —especially in England—its value and prestige suffer from familiarity, for it was made in great quantities for export as well as "home" use. However, a lot of fancy lords and ladies over there still eat off it when it is decorated tastefully enough for them.

Spode and Minton wares are both bone china, as are the Staffordshire and other famous figurines.

PARIAN – When bone china is left unglazed in figurines, it is called parian. But this is also known as biscuit porcelain, and either term will do.

BISQUE – The first baking of any clay (except kaolin, of course) produces a dull, matted surface, and when such pottery is left unglazed it is called bisque, or, if you are very English, biscuit.

Wedgwood is the best-known kind of bisque, and while it can be repaired with epoxy in the same way that any other china can be, concealment of the repair is done with *gouache* paints because they dry to the same matte finish.

FAÏENCE – When a piece of ornamental pottery is glazed with various colors of glass, it is called faïence in northern Europe.

MAJOLICA – Majolica is faïence that comes from Italy, or looks as if it had.

DELFT – Faïence that is made in Holland is called delft.

CLOCKS

(See WATCHES AND CLOCKS.)

CLOISONNÉ

Since ancient times glass has been fused with heat to gold, silver, copper, brass, and iron—but not to bronze, to which it won't stick, or to soft metals such as tin and lead, which melt too soon. Helmets and sword handles, rings, boxes, and jewelry were all decorated this way. But by far the commonest application of this kind of decoration is cloisonné.

In its usual form, a sheet of brass is used as a base, and a design is laid out on it in wires or thin strips of brass. Into each compartment thus formed, powdered colored glass is poured. The whole thing is put into a furnace—*carefully*—and the glass melts and fuses to both the base and the separating strips. The design is then ground smooth and refired to return a gloss to the surface of the glass. Instead, a film of clear glass can be melted over the whole surface.

In use, the surface may become scuffed. In that case the entire surface can be sprayed with clear lacquer from a pressure can. For the most authentic result, use the dull or matte finish lacquer and wax it. You can make the toughest glaze of all with epoxy glue thinned down with alcohol and brushed on with a wide camel's-hair brush.

Pieces of glass that have been chipped or that have fallen out can be replaced with epoxy glue that has been tinted with either transparent or opaque water color. For mixing this material, see CERAMICS.

A product called Ceramit can also be used (see CERAMICS).

COINS

The first thing any expert in the field of coin collecting will tell you about coins is to leave them alone. Do not clean them because the patina on the metal is part of their value. However, there is cleaning that can and often must be done that will not destroy the precious patina.

Gold coins, for instance, though they seldom get dirty, can be cleaned with lemon juice. This is usually necessary when they have been buried in the earth. But if a gold coin has darkened in a box or showcase over many years, that patina is the sort that should not be touched.

Silver coins, though they sometimes tarnish almost black, are what the warnings are really about. They should not be cleaned with anything stronger than mild soap and water, applied with a soft cloth. Not even a brush because we don't want to scratch that patina.

Copper coins should be washed in only the same way that silver coins are washed, unless they have become splotched with green. This is called verdigris and is a form of corrosion, which *should* be cleaned off by soaking the coin in cooking oil for a week and then rubbing the spot with the flat end of a toothpick.

Bronze coins. I know for a fact that in the British Museum they do clean patches of corrosion off ancient bronze coins of Greece and Rome. This they do by painting the good areas with hot paraffin. The coin is then dipped in a 5 per cent solution of nitric acid—which is available from your drugstore because it is used to take off warts.

COPPER

You can do an awful lot of work on a copper antique to successfully restore it to its original appearance. This is because of three things. The first is that you can make it very soft by annealing—so that it is easily reshaped if it has been battered. You can also solder it with soft solder (low heat). And after the old patina has been removed you can create a new patina of the original color on its surface by chemical treatment.

It is like refinishing furniture: You can do such a perfect job that when you are done you have to distress the piece so it will look real.

For example, let's say that you have a weather vane made out of sheet copper that someone has run over with a Model

A Ford. The first step is to anneal it by holding it over a fire until it glows red. This can be done a section at a time, and annealing occurs at the relatively low heat of eight hundred degrees. This is far below the melting point of copper, and having it begin to drip away on you is not a danger. The heat will melt the solder if that was what was used to hold the two sides together. (Sometimes the halves are held together only by bent tabs.)

At any rate, not only will the heating soften the copper so that it is easily worked, you can make it even softer—about 20 per cent softer—if you plunge it while it is still red hot into water. This is best done with a pair of fire tongs held at arm's length—to keep away from the commotion this causes with drops of boiling water flying about. At this point the patina will have flaked off, and any remaining pieces can be scraped off.

Reshaping the metal is then done with a leather mallet or a wooden one with a rounded head on a table that has been padded with three or four layers of a horse blanket or the equivalent. For the finer details, use short pieces of doweling from a half-inch down to a quarter-inch in diameter, whose ends have been shaped appropriately—rounded, cut to a wedge, or to a point.

Next, you solder the piece back together. Use an ordinary soldering iron and the kind of solder with the flux inside. Just because it is easier. (See JEWELRY for more about soldering.)

File off any excess solder and clean the piece thoroughly. Do not use a wire brush for fear of scratches, but kitchen scouring powder is all right. The best thing to use is any metal polish and a buffing wheel on a quarter-inch drill. It's faster and easier. And, of course, after this clean off any traces of polish with a soft-bristle brush.

To prepare the surface for patination, the piece must be boiled in tri-sodium-phosphate, a cleaner often sold in paint and hardware stores. Or you can just as well use Spic and Span, which has t.s.p. in it. In both cases use two cups of the cleaner to five gallons of water. Boil the piece for five minutes and rinse it immediately and well. The cleaned surface must not be touched with your fingers, and the best way to handle it is first to solder a wire to the piece at one of your solder points. This can later be clipped off.

An even patination can be formed by dipping the piece in any acid—starting out with vinegar, which, of course, contains acetic acid. So does lemon juice, but vinegar is a lot cheaper in most places. The dipping will give you a natural-looking brown patina, which gets darker the longer you leave the piece in the vinegar. The process is also speeded up a great deal if vinegar is heated to a simmer—in a well-ventilated spot, of course, for the fumes are unbearable.

You can also get a natural brown with muriatic acid, a 5 per cent solution of hydrochloric acid sold in hardware stores. You don't use a tank. You apply it with a rag wired to the end of a stick.

The best patinas are the beautiful green ones that can form on copper. (Brown forms in smoky cities; green, out in clear country air; and a paler green, by the seashore.) These greens can be made in the following way:

1. Scrub the piece with a rag wetted with vinegar and dipped in a mound of salt. This will turn the copper a smoky red.
2. Immerse the piece in a solution made by dissolving a pound of copper sulphate in a gallon of water. Keep it in a warm place and let it soak for several days.

Different shades of green can be made with other chemicals for step 2. These are copper nitrate, ammonium chloride, iron perchloride, and zinc chloride—all in the same proportion of one pound to a gallon of water. Or use a mixture of any two of them—a half cup of each is usual, but more won't cause any disaster.

Such chemicals can be obtained from chemical-supply houses in major cities. Check your Yellow Pages. Also, you can get them through the jewelers and metalworkers supply catalogue put out by Grieger's, 900 South Arroyo Parkway, Pasadena, California 91109. It's a wonder! (See also BRASS and BRONZE.)

Note: Because copper can be worked so easily when it has been annealed and then made to look old with chemically formed patinas, a whole new school of forgers has crawled out of the woodwork in the last few years. What inspires them to their nefarious practice is the skyrocketing prices being paid for Early American weather vanes, which come in the shapes of horses, cocks, horse and buggies, cows, even early model automobiles. At this writing an automobile vane was recently sold for sixteen hundred dollars.

What these fiends do is to get hold of an original for a couple of days, coat it with grease, and make a mold of it with glass cloth impregnated with epoxy paint. (This is sold mostly for waterproofing the bottoms of boats and customizing hot-rod automobile fenders.)

They make a mold of each side, and then back them up with cement. Into these they then pound sheets of copper that are sold at lumberyards for flashing roof joints and windows. Then they trim the two halves with a pair of shears, solder them together, and dip them in acid. After a little distressing with a chain—making a little dent here and there— only a scientific examination could reveal that they are fakes.

Ah, the simple, honest days of old are gone forever.

DAGUERREOTYPES

In the early days of photography many processes were tried by individual experimenters, but the first to come into common use was the daguerreotype in the middle 1800s. This consisted of a thin piece of copper sheet, plated on one side with silver, with chemicals laid on that were sensitive to light.

The process has turned out to be very durable, though unless the plate is kept under ideal conditions, a tarnish will appear throughout, making the image seem faded and mottled. Happily the tarnish can be completely removed and the image restored to its original bold clearness and detail. It can literally be made to look like new—or as if it had been perfectly preserved over the years.

Perhaps the hardest part of the job is getting the silver-coated copper plate out of its taped inner frame, where it sits behind a protective sheet of glass. The tape, obviously an attempt to keep out the moisture in the air that causes tarnishing, has to be sliced with a razor blade. Once free, the plate must be handled only by the edges, lest fingerprints be recorded permanently in the silver surface.

The first step in removing the tarnish is to wash the plate in mild soap and water. To be safe, use distilled water from your local drugstore. Rinse well, of course.

The ingredients of the solution that will remove the tarnish can all be bought in any "big city" photographic-supply house. And your local photographer will be buying supplies from the one nearest to you. These are:

1 gallon of distilled water
1 drop of wetting agent

¼ ounce phosphoric acid (85 per cent solution)

2¼ ounces of Thiourea

Start with a gallon bottle of distilled water and pour out a cupful to make room for the other ingredients. Then add the other ingredients in any order.

Using a large china bowl or small photographic tray, lower the plate face up in the detarnishing solution, and carefully move the water around by stirring for five minutes. Stir longer if necessary until the image stops improving—without touching the image side, of course.

When the plate is clean, remove it and wash well in more distilled water. Shake off all the water you can, and to hasten drying, douse the plate with grain alcohol (*not* denatured). Just pour a few ounces on the face of the plate from the bottle. Shake this off, and blow the surface dry. Then complete the drying immediately by holding the plate face up over a hot light bulb while continuing to blow on the face every few seconds. You just want the plate to feel warm to your fingers. Do this for five minutes.

Now, reassemble everything, carefully retaping with masking tape, and view with amazement the wonder you have wrought. (See also TINTYPES and PHOTOGRAPHS.)

DOLLS

Water—or even damp air—is the worst enemy of old dolls. We are not talking about ceramic heads and limbs, of course, but the clothing and painted-on features of composition, wooden, and papier-mâché dolls.

If you wash an old doll's clothing in even the mildest soap

and water, there is more than a fifty-fifty chance that you will have committed an act of vandalism. Many of the old dyes have lost their stability. In a purple, for instance, the red might be stable, but not the blue, and so washing will turn the purple to pink.

Dry cleaning, the obvious alternative, is done by immersion. Buy a can of dry-cleaning fluid—at your local supermarket or housewares store—and pour a quart of it in a large bowl. Let the clothes soak for a few minutes, lift them out of the fluid, and let them drip. Repeat the process five or six times. Do not squeeze the clothes, but after the last washing and dripping lay them out on a towel to dry.

Warning: Some dyes will run even in dry-cleaning fluid. The way to test for this before plunging ahead is to take a strip of white cloth, wet it with dry-cleaning fluid, and with your thumb and forefinger press a section of the clothing between the ends of the wetted cloth. If any color comes out of the clothing, it just can't be cleaned unless you are prepared to redye it. This has been done with some dolls.

As doll clothing often has different-colored pieces sewn together, the way to redye it is not with fabric dye but with water colors. Do not use a cheap set because the colors will just fade again. One of the best brands is Winsor and Newton —expensive, but worth it. You start out with the transparent colors, but you can mix in the opaque *gouaches*. The way you work is to dampen the material with water first, by pressing it with a wet sponge. If you are coloring only a sewn-on band or ribbon, wet that, but only with a camel's-hair brush. This pre-wetting of the material allows the applied color to spread out evenly. You can start with a light shade, gradually darkening it as the water dries in the fabric.

Glazed-ceramic heads and other parts are, of course, easily

cleaned. Even the lacquered papier-mâché heads can be cleaned with a damp cloth. And if the features are baked into bisque-ceramic heads, they can even be scrubbed with a toothbrush dipped in Clorox—but test first to see if any of the features are painted on.

Glazed or bisque, ceramic heads are mended and chipped noses and broken or missing arms and feet are restored the same way china is (see CERAMICS). But in recent years reproductions of these pieces have been made in all sizes and shapes, the manufacturers working from the original dolls. They are available from your local doll hospital, of which there are thousands around the country. Just look in your telephone book.

Doll hospitals can also supply you with all sizes and colors of movable eyes and even some wigs, although you can make your own wigs by gluing locks of human hair directly to the head. However, the more authentic way to restore hair is to thread it in little bunches through a cap made of a loose-weave material, touching the underside of the wig with white glue to keep the hairs tight. Also, you will be way ahead of the game if you can get hold of a real human wig—not a cheap one made of artificial hair, but one made of real human hair. You can cut little caps out of this and trim and arrange the hair to suit yourself.

Speaking of hair brings us to dolls with wax heads, where sometimes each hair was inserted individually in the head with a hot needle. More often, a slice was made in the wax and a row of hairs, emerging from the head in the natural-looking direction, was inserted and then sealed in with a heated blade. Restoration is usually done that way.

Repairs to wax heads can be made fairly easily with melted beeswax. If a nose has been broken, for instance, scratch the exposed surface with a needle to remove dirt and with a toothpick apply drops of the wax. When the wax is dry you can sculpt with the broad end of a toothpick that you have given a chisel edge with a razor blade.

Beeswax is usually a pretty good color match, but it can also be tinted with powdered dry colors available at *very good* art-supply stores. Your *ordinary* art-supply store can order them for you.

ENAMELING

I speak here not of a glossy paint but of the original stuff that this paint was invented to imitate. I speak of glass, in many colors, that has been fused to metals, especially iron, copper, and brass. Bronze and steel are too hard. Gold and silver can also be enameled, but of such was the jewelry of kings and queens, and we are not likely to see it outside a museum. In Ireland the Celts were very fond of this form of decoration back around 500 B.C. But it is also found in pieces from ancient Greece and the Near East.

Enameling is also found on your modern kitchen stove, and it was found on the later cast-iron wood-burning stoves—both parlor and kitchen varieties. You can buy kits and kilns to make enameled ash trays in your local arts and crafts store or hobby shop.

The process is a simple one. A clean metal surface is coated with a sticky gelatin, the powdered colored glass is sprinkled on this, and the piece is popped into the oven.

The repair of a metal object decorated with glass cannot be done this way, however, without the original glass decoration running and the patina on the metal being destroyed. The best and easiest material to repair with is Ceramit. This is an epoxy type of very thick paint that comes in many colors and bakes almost as hard as real glass at low temperatures. It is also a perfect glossy match and can be built up in layers. For its use, see CERAMICS.

Moving up in time from the ancient Greeks and Celts to the 1600s in France, we get miniature paintings on clock cases and box tops that were done by painting a hardened layer of white powdered glass with the chemical oxides that give glass its color. After this was baked, another layer of clear glass was baked over it.

If such a piece is cracked all the way through, or the surface has fine cracks, these can be cleaned with a soft toothbrush dipped in Clorox or hydrogen peroxide, alternated.

If a piece has broken out, it can be glued back with epoxy glue.

If a piece is missing and you consider yourself capable of making an oil painting with three-haired brushes through a magnifying glass, you coat the bottom of the hole left by the missing piece with a background of gesso. On this you paint in the missing section of the scene with artist's oil paints, thinned with poppy oil and turpentine for good drying.

You let this dry on a sunny window sill for a week and then fill the hole with clear epoxy. You level the surface of the epoxy with a razor blade after two hours, or sand it level after it is hard. Gloss it with some epoxy thinned with alcohol, and then give the whole surface of the enamel a full-strength coating of epoxy. (See CERAMICS.)

ENGRAVINGS

In its original usage the verb "engrave" meant to cut lines into soft metal to form decorative patterns. It still does. But around A.D. 1500 engraving also became the name for a printing process that flourished right up through the Victorian era until photography and photoengraving displaced it in the early 1900s.

A hard metal tool was used to incise a line in a copper plate. Ink was spread over the plate and wiped off the surface.

A piece of paper was then pressed hard on the plate, and the ink remaining in the lines was sucked up by the porous paper.

The inks were based on boiled linseed oil and/or pine resin filled with carbon, often produced by burning the linseed oil itself. Boiling the oil makes it dry better. The resin is added for substance and for drying. Modern printing inks are still based on these materials.

At any rate, the result is that the ink used in engravings doesn't fade because the carbon is an absolutely stable element. The troubles we run into with engravings are only in the paper: tears, stains, foxing, mold, and mildew. For these problems see PAPER.

ETCHINGS

Etchings differ from engravings in that the copper plate is coated with a wax. The artist scratches his picture into the wax with a needlelike tool. He applies acid to the surface, and where the wax has been scratched away the acid eats into the copper. He then removes the wax, applies ink to the whole plate, and wipes it off. The ink remaining in the etched lines is transferred to paper in a press.

The plate does not have to be copper, for various acids will eat into any common metal. But the same inks were and are used as with engravings (see ENGRAVINGS). For the problems with the paper on which etchings are printed, see PAPER.

FORGERIES

I don't suppose there is anything man has made that some other man hasn't copied and sold for the real thing. The trouble is that this unfortunate aspect of human nature didn't come to the fore just yesterday. Europe is full of fake paintings and carvings made from the eleventh century on—often while the original artist was still alive. So how are you going to tell an imitation Pissarro made the same year as the real one, with the same materials bought in the same places, with a lot of talent, and sold in a shop on the other side of the same city?

You can't. You might say you can, but you can't.

How can you tell a pewter spoon that was cast yesterday in the original old mold and has been distressed and then shined up again? What if it was cast in 1945 and has been tarnishing ever since? You think ours is the only dishonest period and that the fakers weren't busy as bees back in 1945? Well, guess again.

Do you think you can tell if a stained-glass lamp shade is original? What if it was made of pieces of glass from broken authentic shades? And it was pieced together on an original old wooden form? With the strips of copper hand-cut and hand-soldered? With the copper given a deep patina chemically? Then the whole piece painted with a paste made of barn sweepings and then cleaned and polished? Good luck.

Cast-iron toys, mechanical banks, match holders—anything you can think of—are being reproduced today. Art nouveau jewelry, Tiffany lamp bases? Just get a copy of *The Antique Trader*, the weekly hundred-page tabloid-sized newspaper of the antiques trade, and see them advertised openly. To give the publisher credit, these "reproductions" are put in a separate section of the paper, but once they get to the dealer who distresses them a little, how can you tell?

Antique furniture brasses, struck from dies the same way the originals were? You say you can tell them by the regular threads of the bolts that are used to attach them. Nope, even these are cast in molds made from original bolts. Sure, they look new when they come from the factory, but it doesn't take long to fix that up.

They are even faking lithographed Coca-Cola trays from the early 1900s. Ice cream chairs come by the truckload from Chihuahua, Mexico. Bentwood chairs and furniture come by the boatload from Spain. New looking when they arrive, yes. But since they are being made exactly the same way, with the same tools and out of the same materials it doesn't take long before they can be sold as old.

Francis Hagerty, who for many years has been legitimately selling authentic reproductions of Early American antique furniture copied from museum pieces, tells the story of an old lady who came to his showroom one day with an old chair. It was a spindle-back Windsor-type fancy chair with the original paint and decoration half worn off and as dirty as these things usually get hanging around farmhouse kitchens for two hundred years.

The old lady wanted to sell it to him for his collection of originals. He turned it upside down to look at it, and it was one of his. He could tell from a certain detail of the construction. And he could even tell that he hadn't sold it more than ten years before. Another testimony to the well-known fact in the antiques trade that you just can't trust those little old ladies.

Even fine glass and china have been massively faked in

England and sent over to the United States for the last hundred and fifty years. Collectors in these fields know it. But how can you tell the difference, when some freak—who is also a really careful craftsman—takes the trouble to make something the same way it was originally made and uses the exact same materials?

Monetary gain isn't the only incentive these forgers have. It is a part of human nature to get fun out of fooling people. Pompous know-it-all experts, especially, think they are better than we are. That's why I have on my studio wall a Picasso drawing that I made in Spain ten or twelve years ago. It's on a piece of paper obviously torn from the back of a book. The matting, the silvered frame, even the black paper pasted on the back are all handled just the same way I saw it done in the little art galleries in Paris. And everybody believes it is real —even the artists who have looked at it. Someday, after I am dead, it will be sold at an auction. And come to think of it, I wonder how many of those little Picasso drawings we saw for sale in Paris were real? And if you *think* one is real, does it make any difference?

I also have an authentic Windsor chair that I put new legs on, after soaking them in lye and otherwise distressing them. When I show this chair to experts and tell them it is half fake, they always find things the matter with the top of it. I just nod, and tell them how they sure know their antiques.

In a good year more antique French furniture is imported into New York City than was made in the whole eighteenth century.

The world is full of fake Rembrandt etchings, printed on old paper and soaked in coffee. The etchings were made by skillful etchers who didn't just copy originals but used the same windmills and dikes that Rembrandt portrayed.

In the lesser furniture fakes you can tell what they are because the wood shows the marks of machine-planing rather than hand-planing, or circular saw cuts rather than straight, uneven ones done by hand. But what if old wood is used—for instance, attic floor boards from an old house—as it is for the finer fakes? And if the same old hand tools are used?

The list of fakes and forgeries is endless. And what can I tell you that is useful about them? Not much, except that you might collect them for the fun of it. You might even make a few yourself so that you can be amused when the "experts" tell you for the wrong reasons that they are fakes.

Or you might at least buy a book on restoring antiques so that you can fix up battered and broken old ones to look as if they are in perfect condition, and then sell them at an enormous profit. But then you've already done that, haven't you?

FRAMES

There are two kinds of gilded frames that commonly come to the attention of the antiques restorer. As both are covered with gold leaf, they look alike on the surface, but there is a lot of difference inside.

The older and better ones are those made by European craftsmen, going back to the twelfth century—and still being made the same way in a few places. These were first hand-carved out of wood in beautiful detail. The pores were then filled by wiping on gesso, and the surface sanded smooth. Sometimes a second coat was applied, and the surface was then gold-leafed.

For contrast, a dull brown glaze was brushed into the crevices of the carving and then wiped off, and the gold highlights polished. (In artistic terms, a glaze does not have to be glossy, as in common usage.)

In the lesser frames of the Victorian era—and the imitations of the really old ones being made today in Europe— what appears to be gold-leaf carving is really only a plaster cast with a rough wooden frame pressed into it while the plaster was still wet to give it a supporting skeleton, and so some wood would show at the back. Of course, you can tell these imitations immediately by their terrible weight, compared to the real wooden ones.

However, in both cases missing pieces, large and small, are replaced in the same way. In the case of small chip-outs, the old gesso or plaster that has been exposed is first wetted with water and the hole is filled with plaster of Paris. This, when dry, is sanded smooth and regilded. (See GOLD LEAFING.) But for larger missing pieces, you have to cast them, using a corresponding part of the frame as a master for a mold.

There are several ways of approaching this, depending on the intricacy of the carving (or plaster), the shape, and the amount of it that is missing.

If only part of the front surface is missing, you can make a surface mold with waxy modeling clay. This comes in big gray chunks from your art-supply store. You grease a corresponding section of the frame with Vaseline, sprinkle talcum powder on it and blow it off, shape the clay to a roughly corresponding shape about an inch thick, and press it on, working from one side to the other.

Then you pry off the clay, flatten it if the slab has curled, and you have your mold ready to receive wet plaster of Paris. First trim the clay to within a quarter of an inch of the section you want to reproduce, and then fill the mold with only the same amount of plaster as the bulk of what is missing.

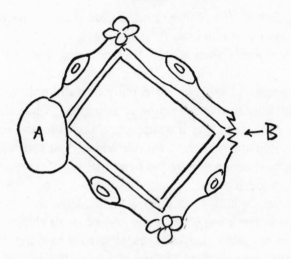

Mat of clay is pressed on good corner (A) *to make mold for casting new piece to be fitted into broken-off corner* (B).

Press the plaster-filled mold into place on the frame, wiping off any excess that squishes out from under the clay.

The plaster should be mixed pretty thick—thick enough so it won't fall out of the mold when you turn it over. Since such thickly mixed plaster has a tendency to set fast, slow it down by using water to which you have added two table-spoonfuls of vinegar per cup of water.

The plaster will still set in ten minutes, but give it half an hour for further hardening before you peel off the clay. Some plaster will stick in surrounding crevices, but you can brush it out with a wet toothbrush.

When a whole piece is missing—as opposed to just the fac-ing plaster—a mold has to be made with liquid rubber, which you brush on in a number of coats or with casting rubber, both of which are available from hobby shops. There is no point in my going on about them, as directions come with them. However, once the casting has been made, its base is going to have to be fitted to the area of the frame from which the piece was broken off—and then attached there.

Epoxy glue and putty will do this well, but first the surfaces to be joined must be sealed with epoxy glue thinned down with four or five drops of alcohol per level teaspoonful of the glue. Brush this on both surfaces to be joined until no more will penetrate and a thin layer remains on the surface. Let this sealer harden overnight, wet them with epoxy again, and squeeze a roll of epoxy putty between them, trimming off any excess putty that squeezes out. The piece will have to be braced in position, of course, while the putty hardens.

Because this is all quite parallel to the way china is repaired, see the more detailed description of this process in CERAMICS.

Touching up can now be done with bronze powders in varnish or wax—as sold in art-supply stores. Or if you want to apply gold leaf, see GOLD LEAFING.

FURNITURE

Since this book is intended for use by Americans and a few other English-speaking people, I refer here primarily to the English styles of the 1700s—the so-called Golden Century of furniture design. These are the charming, unsophisticated styles of Chippendale, Adam, Hepplewhite, Sheraton, and Duncan Phyfe—and in the United States a bastardization of the last three of these called Federal.

They were all designed to suit the taste of the new English middle class of tradesmen that came into being as a result of the expansion of the British Empire and the wealth it brought back to England. Since the taste of these people was limited, it was easy to dupe them with furniture decorated with Greek and Roman motifs that the Chippendale gang dug out of their local library in London. A few acanthus leaves from a Corinthian column here, a garland there, and the yokels snapped it up.

However, in spite of this poverty of creative conception, the care with which these pieces were engineered and the craftsmanship that went into them were superb and are still a wonder to behold. In fact, they were so well made that, except for the effete Hepplewhite, you can still use them two hundred years later. The same is true of the French furniture styles of the period and all the derivatives of both made in the United States during the eighteenth century. But there are many other books in which you can read about furniture styles *ad nauseam.*

Here we are concerned with the happy, simple fact that they were all made of wood. With the exception of the antiqued-white French chairs and small cabinets, they were also, with amazing uniformity, all covered with the same finish: shellac. Stains were rarely used because of the rich colors of the woods: Honduras mahogany, French and English walnuts, and the wood of various old fruit trees after they had gotten too old to bear.

Of course, we have to use stains in replacement pieces to match the darkness these woods have achieved through aging. It is the practice with pieces of museum quality, however, to leave the replacement an obvious shade lighter. Naturally, this practice has also been adopted by forgers to imply more authenticity to their products. (See FORGERIES.)

At any rate, this is the kind of furniture we are going to talk about restoring, though by implication anything else made of wood. This certainly includes all the Victorian styles, which are so meticulously defined in terms of their cultural background in *The New Antiques: Knowing and Buying Victorian Furniture.* *

Restoring Finishes

It seems remarkable to me that for two hundred years—from 1700 to roughly 1900—the same finish was used on all fine furniture. But it was, and it can still be reapplied if you are a bug for authenticity.

This, of course, was and is shellac, a resin exuded from certain trees, mostly in India, when attacked by bugs. It is melted to form flat sheets for transportation, and for use it is dissolved in alcohol—grain alcohol in the olden days but denatured alcohol now.

By modern standards, it is not a very good finish. About all it has to offer is that it is transparent and it can be brushed on when thinned down enough. Its faults are that a spilled martini will wash it right off. Even drops of water not wiped up quickly will turn it white. Left in direct sunlight, it will craze. Left in a damp room over a winter, it will turn foggy.

But it does have one peculiar advantage, and that is that it is easily reamalgamated with alcohol or padding lacquer, the second of which greatly improves the surface by making it much more resistant to spilled martinis and water and totally resistant to fogging.

The first step, of course, is to clean the old finish. Any dirt that is water soluble is first removed by scrubbing the surface hard with a wet cloth and wiping it dry. But more important, usually, is getting off all traces of oil or wax polish. This is done by dousing the surface well with a rag that has been

* George Grotz, (Garden City: Doubleday & Company, Inc.) revised edition, 1970.

dipped in mineral spirits, and then wiping it dry (hard) with paper towels. Repeat the process twice, getting into corners and carvings with an old toothbrush. If the surface is crazed, use a nailbrush over the entire surface. After this is done you need to let the piece dry for only five minutes before proceeding to reamalgamate.

First, the plain alcohol treatment. The surface to be treated must be horizontal. To do the side of a chest of drawers, for instance, you turn it so that the other side is down on the floor. To do the front, you turn the thing on its back.

Now pour a cup of denatured alcohol in a soup bowl, and add a dollop of lacquer thinner. This is insurance against fogging, and a dollop is about an ounce, as in a one-ounce shot glass. This mixture you brush on the surface lightly, just as if you were brushing on thin paint. The shellac will dissolve in only a few seconds, and you will be brushing it just as if you had applied a fresh coat of shellac. You tip off the same way you would with a fresh coat and stop.

You have, of course, used a new two-inch brush, or one that has been used only for shellac and has been well-cleaned with lacquer thinner after each use. Do not use a brush that was previously used for varnish, no matter how well you think you have cleaned it. (More about varnish and brushes further on.)

Your reamalgamated finish should be allowed to dry overnight in a dry room. This means that you must not use shellac in damp summer weather. The best thing to do is to wait until you have turned the heat on in your house. Then the weather outside doesn't matter.

The next day you polish the piece smooth with steel wool, and wax it with a paste wax. If you want a more built-up finish, or if you have brushed the old shellac too thin on some area, spray on a coat of clear dull lacquer from a spray can.

Or, after you have buffed it with steel wool, you can also apply a coat of varnish over the shellac. This usually is done to tops of tables and chests to make them alcohol- and waterproof. (For more on varnishing, see below.)

Reamalgamating an old finish with padding lacquer is the method that professionals use because it is a lot faster. The buffing with steel wool, if desired for a duller surface, can be done in ten minutes. And modern padding lacquers leave a much tougher surface than plain shellac. The trouble is that padding is a skill that has to be practiced.

The padding lacquer is applied directly to a pad about three inches square consisting of about fifteen to twenty layers or old cotton sheeting. This is first wiped and then rubbed harder and harder on the surface as you keep wetting the pad with more lacquer. Or a thin coat of the padding lacquer can first be brushed over the surface you are working on before beginning the padding. This is especially helpful when you are doing a large surface at one time, such as the center or leaf of a table.

But, as I have said above, padding takes a skill that has to be learned on old pieces, which you are going to have to end up stripping. The problem is to learn to work fast and never to allow the pad to stop, or it will stick on the surface, making a mark in the finish that can't be rubbed out. No mistakes allowed. The hard rubbing is necessary to harden the finish with the heat it generates as well as to work the oil out of the lacquer, onto the surface, and into your pad.

And yet . . . once you have acquired the feel for using this pad you can work seeming miracles. Like "refinishing" a drop-leaf table in less than an hour. Or a bedroom set in two hours and fifteen minutes. That is all we used to take when I got my Ph.D. in furniture refinishing by working for the AAAA Patching Service one year in New York City. Our motto:

"Find 'em, Fool 'em and Forget 'em." However, I've told that long and sordid story elsewhere.

Padding lacquer—as everything else mentioned for use in restoring furniture—is available from a fairly magnificent mail-order catalogue put out by Albert Constantine & Son, Inc., 2050 Eastchester Road, New York, New York 10461. They carry everything any woodworking or finishing shop could possibly use: woods and veneers, all kinds of finishing materials, stains, bleaches, an incredible assortment of furniture hardware, and lots more. (Send $.50 for their catalogue.)

Replacing Finishes

Since shellac was the only clear finish used on furniture up until around 1850, removing an old finish is easy. Plain alcohol will do the job, but sticky little beads of shellac might have formed, and they can be hard to get out of corners and carvings. It is far better to use a mixture of half denatured alcohol and half lacquer thinner, which washes the dirty old shellac away beautifully. To apply this you can use old rags or fine steel wool, which you squeeze out in a bowl of alcohol as it picks up the shellac off the surface. Stand the leg of a table right in the bowl while you slosh the alcohol-and-lacquer-thinner mixture up it.

Many pieces made after 1850 can also be stripped this way, but after that date you begin running into some incredibly tough varnishes—some as good as the best we have today. Their toughness seems to come from containing casein. In other words, they are like a thin coating of Weldwood glue, which makes them hard to get off even with paint remover. But TM-4 will do the job.

Incidentally, modern factory-made furniture is not varnished; for assembly-line production it is sprayed with lacquer that dries almost immediately. So most modern finishes can also be removed with a solution of half denatured alcohol and half lacquer thinner. This does not apply, of course, to the companies that make fine—and *expensive*—reproductions of the classical styles. They use real, tough varnish.

One problem you will run into very often is that removing an old finish lightens the color of the piece a lot. This is because of all the dust that was worked into the shellac by polishing it over the years. Sure, the piece now looks the way it did the day it was made, but it doesn't look old compared to the other pieces it has to relate to.

The solution, of course, is to stain it, and the color stain you want to use is walnut. The label on walnut stain may describe it as a rich nutty brown, but it is also the color of old dirt on furniture. And this brings us to a discussion of stains.

The trouble with stains is that they all fade, whether they are made from vegetable matter or chemicals. They fade slowly in a dark room, and it might take you twenty years to notice it. They fade with obscene rapidity in direct sunlight, some of them being completely wiped out in one summer in front of a sunny window. (There are a few exceptions, such as carbon black and the purple from an octopus.)

The worst faders are the clear aniline dyes, which you will know by their being stains that thin with water, alcohol, or lacquer thinner. Of course, they are fast and easy to use. They are strong, they penetrate, and they dry thoroughly in ten to fifteen minutes. So they are used commercially and by most professional finishers to the carriage trade (interior decorators, that is). You can certainly learn to live with them if you will keep your furniture out of the sun. After all, you might not even be alive fifteen or twenty years from now.

But for much better permanence—about three times as good—there are the oil-base stains with finely ground pigment in them. The pigment inevitably settles to the bottom of the can and cakes—but it can eventually be stirred back into the liquid. These stains do not have the strength and intensity of color of the dyes, but that makes them just fine for antiques.

Not only is walnut the basic color you will want to use, it is also the most stable, for there is a lot of black in it. The least stable color is red—as in red mahogany, cherry, and maple. But people have learned to live with faded cherry and maple and to think they are grand.

In applying the pigmented oil stain, you can control the degree of darkness of the color by the amount of oil you mix with the sediment at the bottom of the can. In fact, you can use the sediment straight, rubbing it onto the wood with a cloth pad dipped in the oil as needed for it to move. Then you must let the piece dry for two or three days in a dry room. Do not put it in the direct sun to dry as the oil will bubble up out of the pores in such intense heat and cause spots.

You also have another control over how much stain the wood will take. That is to scuff the surface of the wood with very fine abrasive paper. This will break through the small amount of shellac that remains in the surface fibers of the wood and let the stain penetrate better.

New Finishes

Now we come to applying a new finish. The traditional method is to brush on three coats of shellac, each thinned with an equal amount of alcohol. This means, however, that each coat has to be flowed on very quickly without any re-brushing of an area. On the first coat you can pick up the stain. On the additional coats you can pick up the previous coat, causing blotches. Also, of course, you need at least twenty-four hours of drying time between each coat.

Spray gun operated by cans of "Air."

I think that by now there isn't anybody outside the last back room of the British Museum that isn't using spray cans. These come filled with either glossy or dull lacquer. They look the same as shellac and are a lot tougher. They will not scuff, crack, haze, chip, or craze the way shellac will, and they are far more resistant to water and alcohol—as in spilled martinis. Also, it takes very little practice to learn to use them. The trick is to spray in strokes, releasing your finger from the tip at the end of each stroke and lapping your strokes. Both actions are equal to the same things you would do if you were brushing. Five minutes' practice and you will have the feel of it even on a vertical surface.

The problem with vertical surfaces is to avoid making curtains—just as it is with brushing. To begin with, don't spray your "strokes" from side to side but from the top down. Later, as you get used to doing it, you can do it any old way without worrying about it.

Each coat of this lacquer can be buffed with fine steel wool in ten to fifteen minutes. Then either another coat can be applied, or you can give it a final waxing. If the surface is to be used for eating and/or drinking, a top coat of varnish can be applied over a single coat of scuffed lacquer. We might as well discuss this process right now.

Varnishing

On almost any can of varnish you buy, you will find the statement that it can be applied only over a previous sealer coat of the same varnish. Well, this is just a silly lie told in an obvious attempt to get you to use more of the manufacturer's varnish. It just isn't true, and the funny thing is that if it were true, it would be a pretty sorry varnish.

At any rate, the first thing to do is to choose the varnish you are going to use, and what you want is one that says clearly and outright on the label, with no hedging, that it is made for use on furniture. You DO NOT want one that is intended or can be used for outside trim or on boats or that is "weather resistant." These are the so-called "spar" varnishes, and no matter who tells you a spar varnish is the best, he is just dead wrong as far as furniture goes. The spar varnishes have so much linseed oil in them that they never dry all the way through. These are fine for surfaces that are exposed to summer sun and winter cold, but they are no good on furniture; they never get hard enough for you to be able to buff the surface with steel wool, and they will take an impression from anything left lying on them—from a warm plate, in about thirty seconds.

You want a *furniture* varnish. Next, you want one that says it dries with a dull or satin finish. These are just as good as the glossy ones, and they save you an awful lot of work trying to take the shine off a glossy finish.

Next, you need some mineral spirits with which to thin the

varnish, and a soup bowl to do it in. You pour a cup of varnish in the bowl and add two ounces (two shot glasses) of the mineral spirits. Never put a brush in a can of varnish. If you get some dust on the brush, it will contaminate the can, but a bowl of varnish can always be discarded if anything shows up in it.

The brush you use should be an inexpensive, new two-inch one, unless you are a real nut about keeping brushes clean. The only way a varnish brush can be kept clean is by never being allowed to dry out. That is, between the times you use it you keep it suspended in a can of mineral spirits. If you think I am a nut about this, you will soon learn for yourself through sad experience, for this is the secret of what causes dust specks in varnish. They come not from the air but out of a brush that has been allowed to dry out after cleaning.

To apply the varnish—*always* thinned—brush it every which way, rubbing it right in. Check for any "skips," and then tip it off, holding the brush lightly at a forty-five-degree angle. Then stop. Ignore any brush marks that you can see by looking against the light. They will smooth out by themselves if you will just leave them alone. If you don't leave them alone, the varnish will start setting up, and you really will have brush marks in the dried surface.

Now, even though you have used a dull or satin varnish, in twenty-four hours buff the surface with fine steel wool; following the grain, of course, and after the varnish is good and dry. Then wax with a paste wax.

There is absolutely no need to apply more than one coat of varnish. It will not make the surface any more alcoholproof or wear resistant. Your paste wax is the biggest factor in wear. If for some odd reason you want a thick finish, build it up with coats of sprayed lacquer, which is just as hard as varnish.

Patching

There is only one really adequate way to restore furniture that has been gouged, chipped, or cracked or that is missing small pieces of veneer or inlay, or that has been burned by a cigarette. That is with colored shellac sticks that are melted into the hole, smoothed with a hot blade or specially designed iron, abraded level with the adjoining finish, smudged with stain powders, and then covered with sprayed or padding lacquer.

The first step is to scratch the hole clean with a pointed knife or a single-edge razor blade, and feather (except for a missing piece of inlay, of course).

Shellac sticks come in a basic set of twelve colors, which can be blended to match any color of antique wooden furniture. This is done by heating a palette knife in the flame of an alcohol burner and using it to dig out bits of the stick, which melts easily. Or the stick can be melted directly in the flame and dripped into a teaspoon for mixing over the flame with another color or colors to get an exact match. A basic advan-

Pouring melted shellac stick in hole.

tage of these sticks is that they are the same color in either their melted or hardened state—exactly the same color.

The shellac stick is dripped into the hole, where it is pushed down and leveled off with the palette knife, which you keep at the right heat by constantly returning it to the flame for a second or two.

With fine emery paper wrapped around a small block of hard flat wood, the slight excess of shellac that you have left is then ground level. This has to be done slowly to avoid heating the shellac. Keeping the surface wet with mineral spirits will also help to keep it cool and speed the process.

At this point your patch will have definite edges that will be obvious even if your match to the basic color of the wood is perfect. The professional "polisher," as an expert in this field is called, eliminates the edges by smudging on touch-up powders with a fingertip. He does this with the swift, delicate sureness of a card sharp.

The area is then coated with padding lacquer. When it is dry, in five minutes, it is buffed with steel wool along with the rest of the section of the piece being worked on to get an even sheen, and the section is waxed.

Now, I am quite aware that this is not your casual craft that anybody can do after a few minutes of practice. Frankly, I think that some people could never learn to do it if they tried all their lives. It is the kind of thing that you need to have an inborn talent for, like playing the violin or being able to draw.

Nor are the materials available in your local hobby shop. But if you still think this is something you want to do, everything you could dream of to use in the craft or trade is available from Mohawk Finishing Products, Inc., Amsterdam, New York 12010. But these are serious business people, and not a

Complete furniture-restoring kit from Mo-hawk.

mail-order house, so you have to send $2.00 for their colored wall chart and catalogue and order a minimum of $20 worth at a time. However, consider yourself lucky to have found out about them. It took quite awhile to get them to let me mention their name.

The wall chart is a fascinating work of art in itself. It is in full color. It shows in exact tone and shade 132 different colors of shellac sticks, 157 colors of touch-up powders and stains, and fifty other materials used by professional polishers and at the final touch-up bench in furniture factories. They also have organized these materials into kits, and all their products come with instructions in the catalogue. Their products include a brush-on finish reamalgamator, padding lacquer, stains in spray cans, penetrating stains, aniline stains, burn-in irons for shellac sticks, bleaches, surface polishes and restorers, enamel-repair kits, touch-up stain pencils, and lots more. You have to write to the Amsterdam office to start, but they also have branch stores in Burbank, California; Atlanta, Georgia; Chicago, Illinois; Dallas, Texas, and Montreal, Quebec.

However, if all this is too much for the limited number of

times you need to patch furniture, it is not hard to find someone who will do it for you at a reasonable fee per "burn-in,"
as each patch is called. There are men practicing this craft as
a full-time trade all over the country. They work for furniture
stores that call them whenever a piece of new furniture suffers
the slightest damage in handling. They also make regular
rounds of stores that sell television sets. The big-city furniture
stores even have polishers who work on a full-time basis and
will make evening calls. These men rarely list themselves in
the Yellow Pages, for they are used to getting their work
through the trade. But they *are* everywhere, like a secret soci-
ety. You just have to ask about them at one of the stores they
service.

Distressing

Distressing comes pretty close to faking (see FORGERIES).
But on the other hand, when a really antique piece of furniture is refinished by reamalgamation or with padding lacquer,
it is very likely to come out looking embarrassingly new or so
pristine that it doesn't match other pieces it is supposed to go
with. This would be the case of one chair out of a set of four.
Or a table top that has been refinished and varnish-coated,
but not the chairs that go with it.

Well, as a married man I'm in enough trouble already, so I
am going to leave the ethical aspects of the matter to you.
But if you do decide to distress your new-looking piece, there
are several things you can do to it.

The first is to wear down the finish where any old finish
would be worn down. For this, use a medium-fine steel wool—
such as oo grade—and hit your corners, edges, arms, rungs,
and chair backs with it. With a pointed blade you can replace
scratches where they used to be.

You can get dirt into corners and crevices with raw or burnt umber straight from your oil paint tube. Push it in with an artist's small bristle paint brush and then wipe the excess away with a rag. This will dry in a week, unless you hurry its drying by mixing it with a little drier such as poppy oil or picture varnish. If that is too shiny, brush some powdered pumice into the cracks before it is completely dry, and then brush it and wipe it off until you get the right effect.

Little nicks can be scattered around where they would normally occur by tapping the piece with a screw driver. Table tops can be scuffed where place settings would normally be. Instead of using wax, polish the piece with a dark-brown, oily scratch-remover polish. Sprinkle powdered pumice on this and wipe it off.

If the piece is lighter in color than the others, you should have rubbed it with more opaque stain before you put on a finish. The only thing you can do now is strip it and start all over again. All attempts to stain the finish or spray stain over it and then add a top coat of lacquer or varnish are doomed to failure.

Regluing

Two things cause furniture to get wobbly in the joints. The first is that wood shrinks. And it especially shrinks when an antique that is accustomed to a damp, poorly heated Early American house or soggy English castle is moved into a steam- or hot-air-heated modern house or apartment.

The second is that the romantic old glues that were made from fish heads and horses' hooves and had to be heated in a pot to make them wet were never much good unless they were in a really tight-fitted joint. This is because they softened and gave in damp weather. Modern white glues and a casein glue like Weldwood won't do that. Weldwood, in fact, penetrates the wood and turns into some kind of rock. It is a bit of a bother to have to mix the powder with a little water every time, but Weldwood can't be recommended too highly.

No glue, however, has much chance if you just squirt it into a loose joint full of flakes of old glue and dirt and a little furniture wax and oily polish. To get a good job, you simply must knock the joint apart and clean out the old gunk. To do this fairly easily, first soak the joint or old glue with vinegar, using a brush and pieces of vinegar-soaked cloth. This takes only about an hour before the old glue is softened.

Let the joint dry for an hour before using a modern glue, and if there is any looseness at all, wedge it tight with toothpicks or small, thin wedges of wood. This is basic to regluing a loose rung.

For a loose table leg, put yourself into a calm mood, and turn the table upside down on a carpet. Look at it for a few minutes, and you will see that it is put together quite simply and you should have gotten around to doing this long ago. First you unscrew the screws that hold the top onto the frame. Then the frame—the sides of which fit into slots in the legs—knocks apart easily, and you soon have a simple table kit lying on the floor around you. All you have to do is clean the joints, reglue them, and knock the pieces back together.

Pipe clamps are not really necessary. Just be sure you let the frame dry while it stands on a level floor.

In the case of a wobbly chest of drawers, it is an awful lot of work to take one apart and reassemble it, so I am going to tell you a way to cheat with one of these. What you do is take the drawers out and put the case on its back so you can reach into it easily. Then, every ten minutes for an hour brush hot water into the joints.

This will soften the glue. Now stand the piece up, put in

the drawers, and pull everything together with two tourniquets of clothesline, one about a foot below the top and the
other about a foot from the bottom. Let this dry for about
twenty-four hours, and you will have a tight case.

Now pull out the drawers, which were keeping the case
square, and reglue them. Put them back in to dry, so that they
will also dry in the right shapes. Be sure to wipe off all excess
glue and wax the bottom runners and sides to be sure that
you don't end up with them permanently glued into the case.

Incidentally, the clothesline tourniquets are also useful for
holding the rungs and legs of a chair together when you have
reglued one.

French Antique Finish

While the English furniture makers of the 1700s confined
themselves to simply shellacking beautifully grained and fig-
ured woods, the French and Italians were decorating their
furniture as if their cabinetmakers were frustrated painters,
which they probably were. They coated their pieces with
white or tinted gesso—which you can buy in any art-supply
store—glazed them with various tints of color, gilded them,
glued moldings of garlands of flowers on them, painted
flowers, designs, and even pictures on them—and gilded them
with gold leaf, between the cracks of which peeked a vermilion undercoat.

To touch up such a piece you can use either artist's oil
paints or designer's *gouache* (artist's opaque water colors).
The former will dry glossy, the latter matte, and your choice
depends on what the rest of the decoration looks like. However, after you have restored the decoration, it is a good idea
to give the whole piece a spraying with dull or matte lacquer
from a spray can.

The dull, dusty look in the crevices of the carving is usually quite strong, and this is applied last by brushing on and wiping off a wash or glaze of pumice mixed into wallpaper paste. This doesn't seem very strong but it is only in the crevices, and when it dries it looks like whatever was done originally.

Toward the end of the 1700s—just before Napoleon came along—the basic white of these pieces consisted of heavy coats of white lacquer—actualy powdered chalk mixed in shellac. The chairs, especially, are still being made this way, but now the lacquer is sprayed on. Not only are they being made, they are mass-produced in both France and Italy and are sold in every interior decorator's shop in the world.

Incidentally, shellac sticks come in several shades of white and can be tinted with touch-up stains which come in all the colors there are. They are perfect for patching the chips that commonly appear on these chairs, especially at the joints.

Of course, the modern imitations of these Louis and Directoire chairs are chipped on purpose, besides being spattered with black paint in a stylized form of distressing. I mean that the chips and spattering (imitation worm holes) are done in such a way that they are not supposed to fool you. Distressing has become formalized to the point where it is now decoration.

GLASSWARE

When most people think of restoring glass, they envision a goblet that has been smashed into eighty-three pieces, and they think, "Well, forget it!" It is true that not much can be done about such tragedies. The broken pieces can be glued back together with epoxy glue, but every crack will be clear and sharp, even if you use the techniques for doing this covered in CERAMICS.

On the other hand, lots of things can be done for glass that is dirty, scratched, hazed, worn rough, and chipped, for glass is a material that can be "worked" both by grinding and by working with an acid that will melt it. Not that these aren't delicate procedures, or that you should rush in where angels fear to tread without having practiced first on worthless pieces. Nevertheless, there is no reason we can't all know how these things work.

Cleaning

After being washed in the obvious mild soap and water, glass will retain its sparkle longer on the shelf if it is given a final rinse in a gallon of water to which a cup or two of vinegar has been added. If a glass or bowl has a gold or silver lining on it, do not ever wash it with detergent or ammonia in the water, for this will come off very easily. In fact, you should dry such decoration very gently, because, except in rare cases, the gold is not fused into the glass.

Dullness of glass—from the finest glass to a window pane—is an interesting problem. If it won't wash off, it is not just a persistent film of dirt on the surface. What has happened is that a change has taken place in the molecular structure on the surface. In spite of its brittleness, glass is technically a liquid in a frozen state, and the surface molecules combine with foreign molecules. These can arrive even from gases in the air, but the worst, most obvious, and most frequent ones come from wine.

In any event, dullness and even stains can be removed by abrading them off the surface molecules with a rubbing compound of fine abrasive. This is the way tarnish is removed from silver, and so silver polish is the most commonly available thing to use. Others are jeweler's rouge and stick buffing compounds (sold by Sears, Roebuck, incidentally, and some really serious hardware stores).

Hard hand-rubbing with the silver polish will work in milder cases. Buffing wheels, naturally, are faster. For outside surfaces, a four- or five-inch one can be used. For the inside of a wine glass, your hardware store will sell you a Dremel Moto-Tool, a little hand grinder, for which a speed control is also available. See more about this in CERAMICS.

Surface dullness can also be treated with a pharmacy-obtained 5 per cent solution of nitric acid, which burns holes in clothes and skin. This becomes a problem, because you have to swirl it around on the whole interior of a glass. And after this you have to use the silver polish, too. However, the method you use depends on which way of working you are most comfortable with.

There is a stronger acid, hydrofluoric, which will actually dissolve glass, but this is very scary to use, because even the fumes are deadly. I can't recommend its use unless you have a degree in chemistry. Move back two squares to buffing with rubbing compounds.

Rough Wear

By "rough wear" I mean lots of tiny scratches and chips on a solid glass object, the most common example being a paperweight. I have a friend who used to travel to the northeastern corner of France, where the finest French paperweights were made and still are. They are common possessions among the local people, and he used to buy up the worst-looking ones he could find for a few dollars apiece. Or he'd swap candy for them—with kids, of course.

He would then take the paperweights to one of the factories, where one of the workmen in his off hours would "regrind" them for another few dollars. But this is a very secretive business, and my friend was never allowed to see what was actually done to them. We have speculated that it was first rough-ground, and then washed with the hydrofluoric acid. So here I cannot offer you a quick do-it-yourself method, only speculation. On the other hand, you at least know what can be done if you can find the right craftsman. And just think what fun it would be to take a trip to northeastern France. Beautiful country. From Paris you drive east to Nancy, and work your way south along the Moselle River to Épinal and Plombières-des-Bains and start asking around. Bring a lot of candy.

Chips and Breaks

In restoring glass there is no possible way to mend a break or fill a chip without the repair being perfectly obvious. All we can do is show what a fine piece looked like before it got broken and be as neat as possible.

Of course, we use epoxy glue, and we use one of the brands

that come with both tubes colorless. (Often, one of them is amber colored. To make it more obvious, I assume, when they are totally mixed.) There is an epoxy with two clear tubes in the Atlas Master Mending Kit for China and Glass. For more about this, see CERAMICS, especially the sub-entry on *Porcelain*, which is so much like glass that the mending techniques are about the same.

Perfect cleanliness—a kind of crazy, compulsive caution about it—comes first. Then rehearsal, to include propping the pieces into place. Finally, the expenditure of less glue than you can believe possible. There really isn't any space between two pieces of broken glass that are put back together. None. Any glue will displace them to some extent.

Now, with your fantastically clean (and sensitive) fingertip, you wipe the glue onto *one* side of the break. Then clean your finger, and wipe all but the smallest residue off—trying all the time not to cut your finger, of course. But you do need to use your fingertip because of its sensitivity; only with your fingertip can you feel if there is any glue left at all.

You push the pieces together, as many at one time as you can possibly manage, and set the glass, or whatever it is, in a position in which gravity will best hold the pieces together.

The reason you want to glue as many pieces as possible at the same time—up to three or four—is that if you do them one at a time you run the danger of having a piece set a billionth of an inch out of place, and then none of the rest will fit. Glass doesn't squeeze into places too small for it *at all*. Regarding this aspect of repairing glass, porcelain, and china, pay attention to no one else. People who advise you to glue in a piece at a time just haven't been there.

While I am on the subject of misinformation, do not try to hold setting pieces together with tape unless there is no other possible way. Put your faith in gravity, because it never changes its direction or amount of force. And if any epoxy squeezes out of the crack, wiping it off with a Q-tip is all right if you only have one or two pieces, but it is easier in the long run to peel it off, with half of a thin double-edged razor blade after it has set.

To fill in a chip on the edge of a glass, you can get great results if you put the exact same bulk of epoxy into the hole as there is glass missing, and then suspend the glass upside down while the epoxy sets, hanging like a drop. Large chip-outs and small missing pieces can be built up this way. A delicate business, but nonetheless a workable procedure if you have the time. If such a patch gets too bulky, the epoxy can be sanded smooth. During the sanding, protect the surrounding glass by covering it with tape to avoid accidental scratching. The Dremel Moto-Tool, a hand-held grinder, is perfect for this.

Naturally this leaves the surface of the epoxy dull, but it can be cleared and glossed by brushing a thin coat of fresh epoxy on it with a fine camel's-hair brush. When you do this, thin the epoxy down with denatured alcohol to an almost watery consistency.

New Pieces

In creating glass this way you can also make a mold for pieces more than a quarter inch in diameter, with the help of another section of your piece with the same curve to it. To do this you wax the area of the glass to be reproduced, and then push it down into a soggy lump of plaster of Paris. If you see any bubbles as you look down through the glass, do it over. When the plaster of Paris has set for a couple of hours take the glass off and let the plaster dry another twenty-four hours. Then spray the area into which the glass was pressed with shellac at one-hour intervals until the plaster stops absorbing it. It will dry glossy.

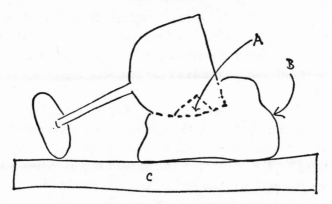

(A) *is area of missing glass inside plaster of Paris mold* (B). *Whole thing is mounted on board* (C) *for tilting to prevent epoxy from puddling in area* (A).

Wax the glossy surface, and now place the glass onto the plaster of Paris with the area of it that you want to replace in the mold. Now brush in your epoxy—full strength—a layer at a time to avoid puddling at the bottom of the hole. The glass and mold can also be attached to a small board so that you can tilt it to keep the epoxy evenly spread on the surface of the mold. This process is made much easier, or anyway shorter, if you use one of the quick-setting epoxies that usually have the words "5-minute" in their names. They may not be as hard as the regular epoxy, but for this purpose they are good enough.

GOLD LEAFING

There is an aura of mystery surrounding gold leafing that is entirely unnecessary. The process, traditionally, began with coating wood with gesso (which is only whiting or chalk or plaster of Paris mixed into any glue) and sanding it very smooth. Several coats might be applied, the top one being a gesso made of powdered colored clay. Dark and vermilion reds have always been preferred, and they have often been left peeking out through cracks in the gold leaf to give it a richer look.

The last coat of gesso was coated with something sticky. Then the gold leaf was lifted with a bushy, camel's-hair brush —made electrostatic by being rubbed on wool—and was dropped on the sticky stuff and pressed down. When a leaf broke, leaving the gesso surface exposed, another little piece was stuck on and pressed down and the whole surface was lightly burnished. The gold used in gold leaf is so soft that at the points where pieces lapped over each other, the burnishing actually worked the molecules of one sheet into those of the other to form an uninterrupted coating of gold.

Such work when done on carvings was then glazed, and rottenstone was dusted into the crevices to give depth to the design. It was never really hard to do, and the sticky stuff that held the leaf on could be a number of things: tacky varnish or paint, tacky shellac for fast workers, even the final coat of gesso before it had fully dried, or just brown glue. Craftsmen's notebooks of other days mention them all. And, of course, any of them *can* still be used today.

However, modern technology has given us two new materials that make matters even simpler. And one that makes it cheaper.

The first thing that makes things easier is that you can now buy gold leaf attached to little squares of tissue paper about three inches square. Originally, the sheets of leaf were just stacked, and lifting one at a time with your dry brush was hard to do without breaking the sheets—pieces of which would blow away if you dared breathe during the process. But tissue-backed, the leaf is easy to transfer evenly to your sticky surface.

And the other new thing is something better than anything used before to make the surface sticky: our "wunnerful, wunnerful" epoxy glue. Epoxy is so great for this because in about an hour the degree of stickiness is just right. Also there is no problem if a drop or two collect in the bottom of a crevice because it hardens internally by chemical reaction. If such a puddle occurred with a varnish, the gold leaf would seal it from the air, and it would never dry. At least it wouldn't dry until you broke the gold leaf while you burnished, letting the still-wet varnish out to make a mess. But once epoxy has set under the gold leaf you can burnish with perfect security.

What makes gold leafing cheaper is that you can now commonly buy a very inexpensive and easier-to-handle imitation of it. It's been known for centuries but used to be very hard to get. After all, gold used to be cheap—only $32 an ounce—and we didn't need the imitation stuff.

The imitation is called Dutch leaf or Dutch foil or Dutch gold or Dutch metal or Dutch whatever. Its composition is eleven parts of copper to two parts of zinc, which when melted together and beaten out into leaf about three times as thick as gold leaf—which is still pretty thin—looks and acts like gold. The only difference is that it will tarnish a little, but the slight tarnish only makes it look like a redder gold. If you don't want any tarnishing at all, it can be prevented by simply coating the leaf with any glaze having a shellac or varnish base. This is almost always done in restoration for an aged look. Instead of applying glaze, you can just spray clear, glossy lacquer on it with your ever-handy spray can.

The main point I want to make about gold leafing is that people think of it as a delicate and difficult thing to do. It really isn't. You don't even have to practice before you do it the first time because there aren't any critical points in the process, and mistakes can be corrected right away. You are just putting fragile sheets of metal onto something sticky. If you are working on carving—as is usually the case—there is no way that you are going to get the first sheet to cover without a lot of breaking that leaves the ground exposed. It is part of the process to take other pieces of the foil and stick them on such exposed spots. The fact that the two pieces of foil can later be burnished together is what gold leafing is all about.

Any mistakes made in your burnishing can easily be corrected by applying another sheet of foil over any area where you have broken through. Examples of double and triple gold leafing are not uncommon on old frames.

A further word about the ground. I have been using the word gesso over and over again without saying why. The point is that it is an ideal ground to apply to a rough surface because it goes on quite thick. A coating a sixteenth of an inch thick is easily managed, and it dries smoothly and can be sanded even smoother if necessary. And smoothness we must have to permit burnishing the surface without breaks occurring in the leaf.

Burnishing, incidentally, can be done with a tight ball of velvet for the appearance usually desired; for a higher shine, use a sculptor's wooden tool or the surface of your fingernail.

On flat surfaces such as glass or tin, no ground is required—just cleanliness and smoothness. When you are putting a strip on glass or on the surface of any other hard object, the sharpness of the edges of your lines is established not by masking but by the stroking-on of your "sticky" with a fine camel's-hair brush. Whether you use varnish or epoxy, it must be very thin, almost watery. After you have laid your leaf on this, don't tamp it down with a soft pad; just blow it down. Then let it dry or set twenty-four hours before brushing off the excess leaf. This is very, very tricky to do with varnish—much easier to do with epoxy—thinned with denatured alcohol, of course.

Finally, a tip on transferring unbacked leaf from the pack to a surface. Just use the electrostatic brush to lift the top leaf over onto a sheet of paper, and then slide it off the paper onto the sticky surface.

GOLD PLATE

Much of research for this book was done in England, because they have been restoring things over there for a long time. And they speak English pretty well, too. While I was there I learned that the English are terrified of two things. One is rabies. They think the streets of the rest of the world are running with rabid dogs and that a bite from one of them means certain death. The other is electroplating.

I think they are afraid of electroplating because cyanide is used in the solution with which gold plating is done, and if the butlers get hold of this they might poison the lords and ladies and maybe even their queen. As a result, you can't buy the solution or the equipment unless you are a registered chemist.

In the United States, however, where we long ago gave up having a king and queen and all that, the materials (and kits) for electroplating are readily available through jewelry-supply houses and hobby shops. If you can't find them locally, you can write for a catalogue to JNT Manufacturing Company, Inc., Stormville, New York 12582.

Gold plate can be applied to copper, brass, silver, nickel, steel, and stainless steel. Whole pieces of jewelry can be plated or replated by dipping. By using an electrified brush, you can replate areas where the original plate has been worn off. Both processes are quite simple, and the only critical area is in getting the piece absolutely clean before you begin and in proceeding immediately thereafter. Copper will tarnish enough in an hour to prevent the process from working.

About the cyanide solution: Don't drink it. It would be absurd to, for it is about as tasty and deadly as lye. Also don't spill or spatter it, because it burns holes in things and people about the same way lye does. So handle it as you would lye. The only thing worse about it is the fumes, which are not always obvious. They won't kill you, but they will make you very sick. So, work in a room with cross ventilation, or under an exhaust fan, or in front of an open window with a fan blowing out of it. In practice these safety precautions apply only to large amounts of the solution, such as quarts and gallons. Jewelers using two- or three-ounce bottles work in normally ventilated rooms, but, of course, they don't inhale deeply right over the bottle.

To plate an article you hang both a small piece of 24-karat gold and the object to be plated in the plating solution. You pass a 3-volt current from the gold to the object, and this moves gold molecules over to the surface of the other metal in about twenty seconds. After that no more gold will be deposited unless you remove the receiving object from the solution, rinse it, buff it, and return it to the solution for a second "plate." Hence, the terms double and triple plating. Each coating looks hazy as it comes out of the solution, but it is easily buffed to the usual glitter of gold.

Cleaning

The easiest way to clean gold plate is, first, to use a jewelry-cleaning dip or a silver-cleaning dip. Then use silver polish, scrubbing the surface hard with an old but stiff toothbrush. Make sure you remove all polish by scrubbing the object under warm water with the same brush. Put the piece aside, and just before immersing it in the plating solution, wash it again in a detergent mixed in hot water. Put it on your drop hook of copper wire (see *Dipping,* below) and rinse it under hot running water. Being hot, the object will dry fast, but absolute dryness is not important.

Electric Current

All you need is three volts of direct electric current, which you get when you connect two flashlight batteries in a series. Actually, the effective range is from two to six volts, and at Radio Shack and similar stores you can get a little transformer for transistor radios that will convert house current (110 volts a.c.) to six volts of direct current. Or you can use a transformer for an electric train set, with the pointer turned to one-third of its range. Because small flashlight batteries are hard to connect, get the large square ones used for camping lights; they have clips on them that are easy to wire.

To the ends of the wires coming from your connected batteries or other source of direct current, attach two small electrical spring clips. Clip the positive (+) one to your gold anode. Bought from a supply house for a few dollars, this anode will be a short piece of copper wire with gold deposited on one end of it. This gold tip *always* goes into the solution first. Just let it hang over the side of the glass jar or ceramic cup holding the solution.

Dipping

The clip at the end of your negative (−) wire is now attached to the top end of the copper-wire hook you have made from which to dangle the object to be plated. Within a few seconds to half a minute of the time you have put the gold-tipped anode into the solution, lower the object to be plated into the solution on the end of the copper drop hook. Hold the anode and the object half an inch to an inch apart for half a minute. If the back of the object being plated doesn't get enough gold on this immersion, buff it with a soft rag or dry toothbrush and on your second immersion turn the un-gilded side toward the gold anode.

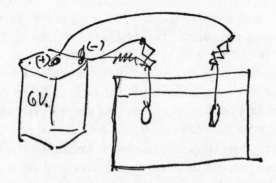

Electroplating by dip method.

Brushing

The JNT Company (see page 91) sells a remarkable little invention with which you can touch up areas from which gold plate has worn off. I think everybody should have one, even if just for the fun of gold plating pennies—especially the big British pennies that recently went out of circulation.

This device looks like a pen flashlight; a wire with a clip on it comes out of the negative (−) end of the two batteries inside, and a brush with an anode hidden in it on the business (+) end. You just attach the clip to the piece to be plated, dip the brush in a solution that comes with the "pen," and brush the surface to be plated without letting the anode (+)

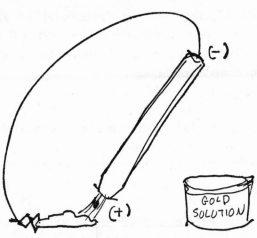

Electrolysis brush containing two 1.5-volt batteries.

inside the brush touch the surface. The trick is that the gold that gets transferred to the object is suspended in the solution in molecular form.

At this writing, JNT will sell you a kit for both dipping and brushing on gold plate for under $25.

GUNS

I will skip right smartly over the question of how old a gun has to be before it can be called an antique. Let your conscience be your guide. The more pertinent question whenever gun collectors gather is whether guns should be restored at all, and if so, how far. On the one extreme are those who contend that every flake of rust is part of history, as in a pistol from a Spanish galleon dug up off the coast of Florida. On the other hand, there are those who contend that all antiques should be restored to their original condition, just as a Chippendale chair is restored for display in a museum. Rust is not part of an original condition.

Well, since this is a book about restoration, we are going to have to go along with the second point of view and cover complete restoration. How far you want to go along this route will have to be your own decision.

Cleaning

A key point on cleaning old guns is to avoid breaking the sharpness of the metal edges of the outside of the case or box. This is especially important where the metal meets the wood of the stock. Also the sharpness of any decorative engraved design. So it is well to avoid using any power-driven wire brush or, for that matter, any brush except where the rust is so thick that it has pitted the surface and already ruined any edges worth preserving.

For even minor rusting, it is best to soak the area overnight in Naval Jelly, a rust remover available in almost any hardware store. Then wipe the gun with clean cloths and polish it with oooo-grade steel wool. If a surface looks as if it could be ground smoother, use various fine grades of emery cloth. For flat surfaces, especially an engraved area, always back the cloth with a small piece of hard flat wood—to avoid breaking the sharpness of any edges, of course. The emery paper can be used dry, but it will work much better if it is lubricated with Liquid Wrench, something of a rust remover in its own right.

The interior works of a gun hardly ever get broken—just rusted and caked with dirt, even when the outside doesn't look all that bad. So 99 per cent of guns that don't work can be fixed by simply disassembling them and cleaning the works. Did I say "simply"? Well, if somebody put it together, there has to be *some* way to get it apart. The first thing, of course, is to remove any visible screws—undoubtedly the most crucial matter in gun restoration.

Screws

With a rusted screw, you just can't be too careful or take less than infinite pains. Obviously, you will pick away any loose rust around the head; then soak the screw overnight in Liquid Wrench. Next, clean the slot with a pointed knife. If it will help matters, the slot should even be squared up with the point of a jeweler's file. A small pointed file such as this can be bought at really good hardware stores; also you can order one from Grieger's, 900 South Arroyo Parkway, Pasadena, California 91109.

Now, you find a screw driver that just fits or is just a little loose in the slot. But you don't use it yet if it is a little loose: first you file the end down until it fits *exactly* into the slot—in fact, it must fit tight, but all the way down, or in. That means that the square tip must touch all the bottom of the slot, and the sides must touch all the sides of the slot. Take your time, because this fitting is crucial.

Next you put the case in a wood vise or clamp it to a heavy worktable so that it won't slide around. With one hand pushing the screw driver down into the slot, you twist it with the other—slowly, and not with all your strength. This is just to test, and see if you are lucky.

If you weren't lucky and the screw didn't start to turn, lay your screw driver aside, and get out a regular-size soldering iron. File the point flat until it is the same size as the head of the screw. Then plug it in and let it get as hot as it is going to get, which will take about five minutes. Put the flat point on the head of the screw for five minutes. In the first minute it will burn out any oil or Liquid Wrench in the area —just blow the smoke away, and continue for five minutes.

When the five minutes is up, disengage your soldering iron, and let the whole business return to room temperature. Put your screw driver in the slot and rap it sharply a few times. *Then* push down and twist, and I guarantee the results. *Unless* half of the head of the screw breaks off! In that event, the only recourse left is to clamp the box to the bed of a good-sized drill press so that a drill can be lowered precisely to drill out the screw. This leaves you, of course, with no screw, and a hole with no threads. But this sort of flat-headed, machine-threaded screw is made in every imaginable size, and a matching one can be obtained from that really good hardware store I keep talking about. (That sort of store is found only in cities of, say, 300,000 population and over, because it is filling the needs of supervising engineers at manufacturing plants.)

When you do find your replacement screw, you set it in with epoxy glue.

Rebedding

When a works case is taken out of a stock, the surrounding wood may be found to be rotten. This you chisel out and replace with a putty made by mixing equal amounts by weight of sawdust and the kind of epoxy sold in kits for repairing auto bodies. It usually comes in kits with glass-fiber cloth, and you get much larger quantities than in the little two-tube packages of epoxy referred to in many other parts of this book.

An exact fit can be obtained by first coating the metal box with a silicon release agent (which comes with the kits or can be bought separately) and pressing it into the putty while it sets. The hardened epoxy-sawdust-putty mixture can be drilled to take screws and can be cut down or smoothed with a metal file twenty-four hours later.

Dents in Stock

Before you refinish a gunstock, the dents in it can usually be raised flush with the rest of the surface by steaming. This is done with an ordinary iron used for clothing. You cover the dent with a wet pad made of about ten layers of sheeting stretched flat on the iron, and apply the iron so as to force the steam into the wood where it will expand the crushed fibers. You don't push hard with the iron. Just hold it tight enough to generate the steam. Or you can let the point of the iron rest on the stock, but don't walk away, because you will have to rewet the pad every few minutes. The process can take anywhere from fifteen minutes to three hours, so don't give up too soon.

One important thing to watch out for is that the sunken surface of the dent is not coated with varnish—sanding of the whole stock may have missed this. But don't try to sand the varnish out of the depression because you will remove fibers from the edge of the hole. Instead, prick that varnish (or whatever) with a pin or needle. A lot. All right, exactly three hundred and seventeen pricks per square inch. Then steam.

Cracked Stock

If a crack has opened up as the result of some impact, it wouldn't have opened unless there had been some tension inside the wood that built up during the drying process. So trying to get a crack back together with glue and clamps is a project doomed to failure.

There are three alternatives. One is to fill the crack with a painstakingly whittled sliver of matching wood that you have to force in—with glue, of course. Another is to fill the crack with a putty made by working matching-colored sawdust (fine) into epoxy glue. When set this can be sanded flush. Or you can put a quarter-inch wood dowel right through the stock, pulling the crack closed with clamps while the glue sets. Then you cut off the end of the dowel flush. Use Weldwood for this and it will never give. (See FURNITURE.)

Checking

Decorative patterns of crossing fine lines "engraved" on a stock look terribly difficult to re-establish if they have been worn or sanded down by some barbarian who worked on the stock before it got to you. But there is a trick. These fine lines are not cut separately but are "raked" in with a tool designed just for this purpose. It looks like a plane blade, except that it has a row of fine sharp teeth on the cutting edge. The tool comes in two standard sizes (number of teeth per inch), one of which will almost certainly fit your lines. You get these from a gunsmith, and you find your nearest gunsmith through a sporting-goods store that sells hunting rifles.

Of course, you can make your own engraving rake by using a small triangular file to cut teeth into the cutting edge of a plane blade. Getting the teeth regularly spaced isn't all that hard if you put the blade in a vise and use a C-clamp to hold a guide to the blade, moving the guide over for each cut. It's no harder than sharpening a saw, and everyone has done that —haven't we? Besides, what better way to spend three or four hours on a cold, winter evening listening to your TV set and just looking up for the good parts.

Oil Soak

Many people who use rifles pour oil into them after each use and leave them standing stock down. A stock sometimes gets so soaked with oil that it turns almost black and you can't see the beautiful graining and figure of, say, a Circassian walnut stock.

The best way to remove this oil is to dismount the stock and hang it, oil-soaked end down, over a wood stove for a winter. Hang it close enough so that it will get really hot by the time your first flapjack is cooked in the morning.

You can also keep your stock on top of a steam radiator for a winter, or even bake it in your oven at a low temperature for a couple of weeks.

Finally, you boil the whole stock in a solution of four cups of t.s.p. (tri-sodium-phosphate) to a gallon of water. T.s.p. is used as a brush cleaner and in paint-removing tanks, and so you can get it from stores that supply house painters—in other words, wholesale paint houses. You can also find it in some better paint and hardware stores. A good substitute is Spic and Span, because it has a bunch of t.s.p. in it. Don't worry that this will hurt the wood, because it won't.

Let your stock simmer for about twelve hours. Then rinse it, wipe it dry, and let it air-dry at room temperature for a week.

Finishing

As the stock dries you will notice that a fuzz has appeared on the surface. You can best remove most of this with ooo-grade steel wool. Then smooth the wood with very fine garnet paper. It is now ready for finishing. To see what it is going to look like with a finish, wet it with mineral spirits. If you want a darker color, mix up a stain with a color ground in oil. Oil-based tinting colors are available in any paint store. (Burnt sienna darkened with burnt umber is a basic gunstock color.) You thin the color with boiled linseed oil, and rub it in with your hands.

A linseed-oil finish is standard for gunstocks, because it gives gun owners something to do once a week out of hunting season. You just rub in another coat with the palms of your hands until a finish builds up on the surface of the wood. It's a good finish, and it does have a nice smell, and besides the advantage of keeping you busy, it takes about a year of weekly rub-ins.

A better finish is a penetrating wood sealer of the kind used for basketball courts. Just ask at your local high school for their source. Apply one coat to penetrate—soaking it in until the wood won't take any more—and then one coat twenty-four hours later to rest on the surface. Smooth each coat with oooo-grade steel wool when it is dry, of course. Then apply a paste wax.

If all this sounds like overrestoring to some of you purists out there, I think so, too. But as I said in the beginning, all the restoring you can do is what this book is about. So use your own discretion.

IVORY

Ivory is different from everything else. Its fine grain and softness makes it incredibly good for intricate carving. It is basically elastic, and it is this quality that gives it the feel of ivory. Ivory also has a high water content, which can be lost— causing it to split and, if the ivory is ancient, to powder. All these qualities are due, of course, to the nature of its source: mainly the tusks of elephants and walruses. Also of hippopotamuses and narwhals; a narwhal is a Delphinidae cetacean, a sort of sea-unicorn, which lives in arctic seas. Actually, a narwhal has two teeth, but usually only one of them develops into a spiral, straight horn. Finally, there is Russian ivory, which comes from an extinct species of very big elephants whose tusks are still dug up in Siberia from time to time.

All that erudite stuff aside, the reason that ivory splits is that it has the same internal structure as a tree trunk. It is built up in concentric growth circles and a cross section will tell its age. Excessive drying causes a tension because the outside rings dry faster than the inside ones, causing the outside to split. (Wood splits for the same reason.)

In the case of ivory, however, when it is put in normally humid air, it will absorb enough moisture to swell up and close its crack. For this reason, cracks must *not* be filled with anything hard. The traditional filler—and none better has yet to be discovered—is beeswax and paraffin in an approximate fifty-fifty mixture. The two are melted together and filled with enough whiting (powdered chalk) to make the wax opaque. Since the beeswax has a tannish color, this will sometimes be a close color match to the ivory. Or powdered ocher can be added to darken the color. Ivory, incidentally, darkens naturally with age, and so you never bleach it.

In fact, you don't even wash it with water, except for wiping it with a damp cloth. The correct cleaner is mineral spirits, and even that is just brushed on and quickly wiped off. In the case of carvings, you must first test to see if the mineral spirits will wash out any of the brown stain or glaze in the crevices. This stain was often applied when the piece was made, to give depth to the carving. Even if it is grime, it is antique grime—as in the case of *netsuke* carvings—and should be left alone. If it is accidentally removed, you replace it. This you do by applying a glaze of beeswax thinned a little with mineral spirits and colored with raw umber and/or burnt umber in powder form. You allow the glaze to dry for a few hours and then wipe it off with a soft cloth.

When the ivory handles of knives loosen, it is obviously because somebody was foolish enough to wash them in nice hot soapy water. This caused the ivory to expand and contract, and it also softened the wax, tar, "hot" glue, or solid shellac that was used to mount the blade in the handles in the first place. Antique handles, in other words, were always mounted by something that you could melt and that would harden on cooling. This method is still used with French chefs' fine knives. A hole is drilled into the handle and filled with melted stick shellac loaded with sand. The handle end of the knife blade, which is just a pointed spine, is then heated enough to melt the shellac and pushed in.

Of course, you can use the same process to remount an ivory handle. But if it is a fine antique to be displayed and not used, the correct material to use for such a remounting is pure beeswax because it will give with any expansion or contraction that should take place in the ivory.

In the case of a really fine and very old piece of ivory that has begun to deteriorate, the modern method of restoration is to impregnate the area that has begun to powder and crumble with one of the modern white glues such as Elmer's. This glue is preferable for ivory because it has a certain amount of elasticity when dry. (See TEXTILES and LEATHER.)

For this purpose the glue is thinned about 15 per cent with water and applied with a dropper, any excess being drawn up with a soft camel's-hair brush.

When a piece has been broken off a carving, it is also glued back with white glue. If the piece has to be replaced, the area is built up with drops of melted beeswax, tinted with dry color to match, and then carved.

JADE

The term jade applies to a whole family of stones that polish to an oily-looking translucence. The color ranges from pale gray through all kinds of greens and blues to a greenish black. Its soft appearance is deceptive for a sharp edge of it will scratch glass just as a diamond will. The only way it can be carved is by grinding it with fine abrasives.

However, jade does fracture, and in that event it is restored the same way porcelain is. See *Porcelain* under CERAMICS. Also see GLASSWARE.)

JAPANNING

Although the word japanning is used loosely (if wrongly) for any shiny coating on wood, especially in furniture, it is specifically an imitation of Chinese and Japanese lacquerwork in which asphaltum is used as a substitute for true lacquer. It is a process that became very popular in the mid-1800s.

Japanning calls for some definitions. In antiques usage, lacquer is the same thing as shellac. Both are the various tree resins dissolved in alcohol. The only difference is that if it comes from the Orient, it is called lacquer, and if it comes from Europe, it is called shellac. Also, in the Orient it was commonly loaded with dry pigment, especially red and black, while in Europe it was commonly used as a clear finish for wood. However, in the 1700s the French took to loading their shellac with all colors of pigment, too—therefore producing exactly the same product that had been coming from the Orient in the preceding century.

In the early 1800s, however, it was discovered that a cheap imitation of lacquerwork could be made with asphaltum, a brownish-black resin found in mineral deposits. The asphaltum was dissolved in linseed oil and turpentine—as opposed to alcohol for shellac and lacquer—producing what we would now call a varnish. This meant that it had to be smoothed with pumice and then oil-polished to get its shine.

On the other hand, the lacquer of both the Orient and France was French-polished with pads soaked in oil to bring it to a far glossier state. (In French-polishing, the heat generated by the pad—or the palm of a hand—softens the surface of the shellac so that it becomes as smooth as glass.

So, in restoring japanning, we are dealing not with a lacquer but with a coat of polished black paint. In furniture it is almost always on a white gesso ground (see GOLD LEAFING)—which has cracked. On tin trays, water had gotten under it in corners to rust it off.

The cracking of the gesso panels on furniture is due to shrinking of the wood and loosening of the joints. This has first to be corrected by regluing the whole piece. The cracks in the gesso can then be filled with any paste wood filler or plaster of Paris.

For touching up your repairs, you can, believe it or not, still buy asphaltum paint from good art-supply houses. Its color can be modified with artist's oil paints, and you smudge it with your fingertip to blend it into the base. To obtain an even gloss, you spray the whole panel with gloss lacquer from a spray can. If this doesn't look antique enough, dull it with 0000-grade steel wool and wax it.

The same process applies to japanning on metal. Just be sure you grind the rusted surface really smooth before you begin. If the metal is pitted, you should fill it first with spackle or a fine-grained surface filler such as white Duratite.

JEWELRY

For cleaning jewelry, see GOLD PLATE, *Cleaning*.

For restoring jewelry by electroplating, see SILVER PLATE and GOLD PLATE.

For resetting loose stones use epoxy glue (see CERAMICS).

What we are going to consider here is repairing jewelry by the subtle art or craft of soldering—and, by obvious extension, the soldering of other objects made of precious and common metals such as silver, gold, copper, brass, iron, and steel. (Old steel, that is, not the modern stainless and super ones, which can't be soldered but aren't antiques either.) For soldering is what the making and repairing of jewelry is all about. It is the way antique jewelry was assembled. Soldering will also repair broken metal objects from ancient times.

The essence of the process is that two pieces of metal are "glued" together by a metal that melts at a much lower temperature than the pieces to be joined. The two pieces don't even have to be the same kind of metal—just so long as they both have higher melting points than the metal used as the "solder."

However, there is a little more to it than that because over the years two kinds of solder were developed: hard solder and soft solder.

Hard Solder

Hard solder is also commonly called silver solder, because silver is the main ingredient. But to make it melt at a lower heat than the silver and gold it is commonly used on, copper and zinc are added. Used in various proportions, these give silver solder an average melting point of around 1400° F. (By comparison, soft solders melt under 400° F.) This high heat creates a fantastic bond. The molecules of the solder penetrate the surfaces of the silver or gold pieces so joined, truly fusing them, so that such joints cannot later be unsoldered.

Because of the high heat needed, silver soldering must be done with blow torches, ranging from the kind that are affixed to small cans of propane gas to the fine-pointed torches that combine oxygen with the gas. Typically, the two pieces to be joined are iron-wired together with thin strips of the solder between them. Or they are held by special clamps designed for this purpose. The torch is moved back and forth over both pieces until they reach a heat where the solder between them melts. The torch is then withdrawn before it melts the pieces.

Ronson Varaflame torch adjustable for both hard and soft soldering of jewelry.

Such work is, of course, the province of someone who has been trained in jewelry making, although there are many courses given for those who wish to take up the craft as a hobby. At any rate, given that you have some source of instruction, all the materials and tools are available from a mail-order house catering to amateurs and professionals alike: Grieger's, 900 South Arroyo Parkway, Pasadena, California 91109.

Soft Solder

Soft soldering is a craft that can quickly be mastered by anyone who is "handy," and the materials are both inexpensive and readily available from hardware stores and craft shops.

The principle is the same, but since the heat used is so low, it can be applied with a soldering iron with little if any danger of ruining something by melting it. (Except pewter, for which see PEWTER.)

Soft solders are made of varying mixtures of tin and lead, usually 60 per cent tin to 40 per cent lead, which mixture has a melting point of 360° F. (much lower than pure lead's melting point of 621° F.). Such solders can be used to join old steel, wrought iron (but not cast), silver, gold, brass, zinc, nickel, and copper and its alloys. Also, they can be used on lead and pewter in theory, but with a danger of too much heat causing disaster. After it has cooled, soft solder can easily be filed down with fine "jewelers' files" and polished smooth with emery cloth and finally silver polish. It is a very usable process for anyone who will practice for just a few hours to get the feel of it.

Step by step, it goes like this:

The Soldering Iron

Although the small-sized iron you can find at the hardware store will do, you can get a nice little pointed one at a hobby shop. The end that gets hot is copper, and for each use you should clean it with a file and fine garnet paper, trying to wear away as little of the copper each time as possible. Before each use it should be wiped with a little flux, which you buy at the hardware store in a tin can. Both actions will keep the point from crudding up, and the solder will flow better off the point. It gives you far better control than a dirty, unfluxed point.

Cleaning

The surfaces to be joined should be scratched or abraded clean. Scratching is best when the metal is soft enough because it gives the solder more "tooth." Then you immediately coat the surfaces to be joined with flux, using a fine camel's-hair brush, if necessary, to be sure you get the flux only on those surfaces. That is part of the trick of neat, easy soldering. When heated the solder will flow to the fluxed surfaces, while it tends to run off the surrounding unfluxed surfaces.

Clamping

Ingenuity is called for here. As mentioned for silver soldering, the two pieces can be tied together with iron "stove pipe" wire. But they can also be pushed together—say, with bricks. Or held together with small spring clamps. Or you can make a wooden jig by nailing little pieces of wood to a board.

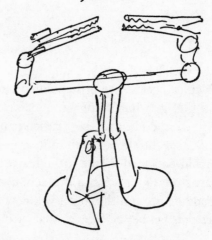

A holding jig for difficult soldering and gluing jobs.

Soldering

First you hold the soldering iron with no solder on it to the joint to heat up the metal on both sides of it. Now apply a little solder to your already fluxed copper point and touch it to the joint. It may flow right in. If it doesn't, just hold the point there until the metal gets hot enough to suck it in. Just experiment, and you will get the feel of it quite quickly.

There are also a number of products consisting of finely powdered soldering metal mixed to a paste with flux. They come in a tube and can be applied to the surfaces to be joined instead of flux. Then you just heat the joint with the point of your iron. But I have never found them to work any better than the basic method.

There are also on the market some products claiming to be "low-temperature silver solder." Well, that they may be, and I am here to testify that they certainly work just as well as the tin-lead solders, but the only advantage that I can see in them is that they are a brighter color. In some situations they are too bright, and ordinary tin-lead is a better color match.

Finishing

Obviously, anything that melts under 400° F. is going to be an easy metal to work. You can even scrape off any excess with a hard, sharp knife point. Of course, it files off very easily with a fine file, too. Even a nail file is good. But since the metal is so soft, it quickly clogs the file. To prevent that, just rub plain white chalk on the file from time to time, and clean it with a brass brush of the kind used for cleaning suede.

The metal surface can also be rubbed with fine emery cloth; for a glitter, it can be burnished with any smooth steel surface, such as the side of a knife blade or the back of an ordinary silver-plated or stainless-steel spoon. Small burnishing tools designed for just this purpose can be bought.

Now all you need to do is buy up some old broken pieces of jewelry so that you will have a sort of junkyard in which you can find parts for repairing the better pieces that come your way.

LACQUER

In modern usage, lacquer is the finish sprayed onto factory-made furniture as it comes to the end of the production line. It is a product of our chemical industry, and while not as resistant to spilled liquids as varnish, it is pretty good; it dries in a matter of seconds—and that last quality is what counts at your friendly local furniture factory.

But in the "wunnerful" world of antiques it means a very shiny finish on small boxes, large boxes, and some very spiffy Oriental and French cabinets.

The way you lacquer is this. You start with a wooden base, and give it a coat or two of gesso, which you polish very smooth with fine abrasive paper. Gesso is any fine white powder made into a thick paint with any animal glue. The powder can be chalk, whiting, plaster of Paris, or any powdered clay. This surface is then French-polished with shellac to which colored pigment has been added. In China and Japan, where this process has been used for many centuries, the colors were usually black, vermilion, and a deep red that has become known as Chinese red. In France, where the process was used for the styles popular there in the eighteenth century, pastel shades of blue and green were most common.

In the French-polishing method, the shellac is applied with a pad of cloth, three or four inches square, that is wetted with linseed oil—with which the shellac will not mix. The shellac is rubbed on in nonstop figure-eight strokes lest the pad stick to the finish. This rubbing is hard enough to generate just enough heat to keep the shellac soft, so that being rubbed fast with the oily pad brings it to a glossy mirror finish. (This is sometimes toned down with abrasives or glaze, especially in the French things.)

If it sounds as though I am saying that—in terms of antiques—shellac and lacquer are the same thing, you are following me perfectly. They are both the same kind of tree resin dissolved in alcohol. The only difference lies in the means used to apply it. Brushed clear on a Chippendale chair, the resin is a shellac finish.

Colored with pigment and rubbed on with an oily pad, it is lacquer. And, come to think of it, rubbed on *clear* with a pad, it is called a French-polish finish, which is commonly found on French-style fancy chairs and old-time pianos and other handmade wooden musical instruments.

For the difference between lacquer work and japanning, which is an imitation of it, see JAPANNING.

LAMPS

If you want to drill a hole through the bottom of your Ming vase (Ming dynasty, 1368–1644) to convert it into a lamp, that is none of my business and I don't even want to hear about it. So I won't tell you what you have to use to avoid splintering it is a carborundum drill—which is, in essence, a pointed grinding stone. It is what you would also use for glass bottles and fine old French porcelain.

But barbarians aside, there are many kinds of fittings that can be used to convert *objets d'art* into lamps without ruining them. There are also various kits for electrifying old kerosene and oil lamps of the American Dynasty (1812–1914). They are all available at wholesale, to antique dealers, from the Brown Lamp Company, Box 12511, Creve Coeur, Missouri

63141. In their catalogue, you will also find 139 other items in various sizes and shapes. Send one dollar, and ask for their *Lamp Parts* catalogue and the name of the nearest dealer.

In it you will find, for instance, spindles, nozzles, arm backs, bracket caps, knobs, finials, candle cups, swivels, spacers, shade raisers, check rings, couplings, necks, vase caps, harps, thirty-three different kinds of sockets, and so on and on with the hardware. But also you will find reproductions of antique reflectors, many kinds of glass shade reproductions, twenty-four sizes and shapes of lamp chimneys, hurricane chimneys, and all kinds of fixtures and brackets for hanging lamps of the various periods. Not to mention the funny flickering bulbs that are supposed to look like flames and make me a nervous wreck whenever I am in a room with one of them.

This is not a paid advertisement for the Brown Lamp Company—I just consider it useful information.

LEAD

Pure lead melts at 621° F., and so it is possible to solder it with an ordinary soft (tin-lead) solder that melts at the much lower point of 361° F. But very carefully. And not with a soldering iron as a source of heat, because just the touch of a too-hot iron will cause a disaster. Instead, a piece of solder hammered flat is put between the surfaces to be joined— fluxed, of course—and the whole area is gently and slowly heated until the solder melts. For more particulars about the process of soldering, see JEWELRY and PEWTER.

The only common antiques made of lead are cast garden

ornaments and urns in which flowers are planted. When these are in the middle of Victorian lawns and in cemeteries, they develop a natural patina in the atmosphere.

To clean a piece such as these without disturbing the patina, wash/scrub it with Spic and Span or tri-sodium-phosphate from your paint store. If the patina has been removed, and you want to restore it in a hurry, brush it with muriatic acid (a 5 per cent solution of hydrochloric acid), which you get at a hardware store—where it is sold, basically, for cleaning lime stains from bricks.

That is for the natural dark gray patina. Lead can also be made to look like copper by being given an artificial green patina. That was done regularly in the Victorian era. To do this, prepare the following solution in a three-quart glass bowl or enamelware pan: *First,* put in one quart of water. *Then,* add a half cup of vinegar, two ounces of copper nitrate, and one ounce of ammonium chloride. Both chemicals are available from chemical and jewelers' supply houses.

The solution is heated to a simmer and brushed on with a scrubbing motion. (Of course, any old patina must first have been removed with a wire brush or steel wool until the lead shines brightly.)

LEATHER

In addition to the leather bindings of books (see BOOKS), leather is often found on boxes, old screens, and panels, often painted and decorated with gold leaf. And then there are the hard-leather objects such as fire buckets and firemen's and soldiers' helmets, for which the technical term is *cuir bouilli.*

We have to rely on the French term for it, because there isn't one in English. And, of course, there are all the harnesses, saddles, cases, trunks, and upholstery.

The chief problem with all these things—except the *cuir bouilli*—is that leather tends to dry out very easily. It then becomes hard and brittle and tends to curl and flake and fray, even powder.

The basic way to restore such leather is to impregnate it with something very close to its original natural oils, namely, lanolin, a chloresterin-fatty matter that comes out of the skin of sheep and is boiled out of their wool.

It has been found that this treatment can be made to remain effective indefinitely if beeswax and a little neat's-foot oil are added—with some benzene or mineral spirits for a solvent. This is known as British Museum Leather Dressing, because that is where it was developed and from where it was given freely to the world. Although the proportions need not be exact, those suggested are: 7 ounces of lanolin, ½ ounce of pure beeswax, 1 ounce of Cedarwood oil (neat's-foot oil can be substituted), and 11 ounces of benzene.

The first step in preparing this mixture is to melt the beeswax in the benzene; this is quite hard to do on a stove without burning your house down. What you do is to shave the beeswax as thin as you can with a knife or potato peeler, put it into a one-quart glass jar, add only a cup of the benzene (or mineral spirits), and heat this in a pan of water. Start with warm water and slowly bring it to a simmer.

Once the wax has been dissolved, you can turn off your stove, move the jar to a table, and gradually stir in the rest of the thinner. (This way you have never had more than a cup of the benzene near the fire.) Then add the lanolin and the oil.

This dressing should be soaked into the leather three or

four times at twenty-four-hour intervals for maximum effect.
The effect, of course, is to make the leather supple again.

If, however, you have a piece of leather that is literally falling apart, and you just want to hold it together, the standard
museum practice is to gently drip melted paraffin on it. You
can obtain melted paraffin by melting down plumbers' can-
dles or you can use the paraffin sold for topping jars of homemade jelly. Twenty-five per cent beeswax can be added to the
paraffin to stiffen it further.

Most stains in leather—*all* those caused by water and ink—
can be removed with a mild solution of oxalic acid. Say, a 25
per cent solution. The way you obtain this is to start with a
pint of hot water in a quart jar and add the oxalic acid crystals (from a hardware store) until they stop dissolving and you
have about a half inch of them on the bottom of your jar. Let
this cool, and you have a saturate, or 100 per cent solution.
Add one part of this to three parts of water, and you have a
25 per cent solution.

Do not apply this just to the stain you want to remove, but
brush it onto the whole piece or section. Then use a camel's-
hair brush to add some of the 100 per cent solution to the
stained area. Let this dry thoroughly, at which point the
leather will be covered with a fine white dust that will make
you sneeze. But wipe it off well with a damp rag and let the
leather dry again. Then apply British Museum Leather Dressing and/or a paste furniture wax.

Leather panels have to be removed from any backing—
usually wood—before they can be treated from behind with
our dressing to soften and preserve them. They can almost always be removed with water, but the water must come from
behind, too, or the painted decoration could be destroyed.
The usual way is to lower the panel into a large pan of water,
supporting it from below with wedges so that the wood is half

immersed but the leather stays a quarter inch above the level of the water. The pan is then covered, and the soaking is allowed to go on for a week, or as long as it takes until the leather can be lifted.

When leather is to be glued to itself or to cardboard or wood, scrape the back of it as clean as possible and use white glue—because of its elasticity.

Hard-leather objects often fracture and are best repaired with epoxy glues. For the use of this, see CERAMICS.

LIMESTONE

Limestone is a coarse form of marble. Looked at from the other end of your Pietà, marble is limestone that has been crystallized by pressure and heat in the bowels of the earth. And since this crystallization is a gradual process that occurred in varying degrees, there is a whole range of varieties of stone between what is obviously limestone and what is obviously marble. There are lots of shades of color in them all because of the presence of traces of mineral oxides in the hundreds of sedimentary deposits of limestone/marble that are found all over the world.

In popular usage, limestone is the gray to yellowish-gray, sandy-surfaced stone of which garden statues are commonly made. It has also been used for statues indoors and out since ancient times. The limestone statues were chipped out of solid blocks of the stone and then polished. When they are weathered they look as if they could have been cast with cement containing a lot of fine sand. They well might have, because the way you make cement is by baking limestone. The resulting powder is then mixed with varying amounts of sand of different degrees of coarseness for pouring into molds to make statues.

Naturally, the way you repair a limestone statue that has been broken is by using a paste of pure cement as the glue, first scratching and scoring the two surfaces to be joined. You can also add dry colors, sold in good art-supply stores, to tint your cement to get an exact color match. Of course, after adding any color to a test batch, you have to wait forty-eight hours to see the color that results when the batch is dry. Determining how much of which color to use can easily take a couple of weeks. But you know the old French saying: "Antique restoration is the art of ridiculously patient people."

Besides being glued back together with cement, broken statuary is also sometimes doweled when greater strength is needed—as in the reattaching of an outstretched arm that has been broken off. It is done with pieces of quarter-inch brass rod, with pure cement as the "glue." (No sand in it.) The holes for the dowel are drilled with an electric hand-held drill and a masonry bit. Of course, the size of the dowel you use depends on the size of the piece. It can be as big as one inch in diameter.

Because of the difficulty of getting the dowel holes in the surfaces to be joined exactly opposed to each other, one of them can be drilled larger than the dowel.

Replacement of pieces broken off antique limestone statues is, in certain rarefied circles, a matter for hot debate. Many people—especially English museum people—think that if Nero has had his nose knocked off, only the lowest-class peasant would replace it. Yet we have evidence that such repairs were made a couple of thousand years ago when breakage occurred.

Of course, if any of you low-class peasants out there want to do this sort of thing, it is quite easy. And it is certainly done all the time to Victorian garden statues—even in England. Cement is the medium, with enough of the right coarseness of sand in it to match the texture of the surrounding area.

As mentioned above, this can then be colored with dry colors, including white. You can even buy a white "topping cement" in small packages at a good hardware and paint store to start with.

Cleaning

If limestone or any stone carving still has a polished surface, you should try to preserve this when cleaning it. Mineral spirits and a bristle brush of the kind used for kitchen cleanup are perfectly safe. Then plain soap and water, but not ammonia and not t.s.p. or products (such as Spic and Span) containing it.

Of course, if the surface has gotten rough and pitted, in addition to being filthy, you might as well go right to it with both the ammonia and Spic and Span.

Then, after a very good rinsing, let the piece dry—for forty-eight hours inside a warm, dry house or for a few dry, sunny days in summer or fall if it is outside. You can preserve it from further deterioration by coating it with paraffin or beeswax or a mixture of both. A fifty-fifty mixture is the most popular. You melt the two waxes together in any old pot, take the pot away from the stove, and thin the waxes down by adding 10 to 15 per cent of mineral spirits or turpentine.

You brush this on the statue or carving, which preferably is warm. On cool or cloudy days you can warm the stone with one or more electric radiant heaters. How thick a coating of wax you want to apply is a matter of preference. Unthinned, it can even be used to fill pitting in the surface. At any rate, let it dry for a few days after application so that it will get hard enough by evaporation of the spirits to take a good shine with soft rags.

For removal of stains from limestone see MARBLE.

LITHOGRAPHS

Lithography is a process of printing from chemically engraved limestone that was invented by a German in about 1796 and has been used by artists for limited editions of prints ever since. The reason they like it can easily be seen in the widely reproduced lithographic prints that Toulouse-Lautrec made as advertisements for Paris night clubs.

In lithography the artist draws directly on a polished slab of limestone with a waxy crayon. When he is done, he pours nitric acid on the slab; this eats into and roughens the stone wherever it isn't covered with the wax.

After the acid is rinsed off, the stone is kept wet while printing ink is rolled onto it. The ink does not stick to the wet roughened areas but does stick to the glassy-smooth areas that the wax has protected from the acid. A piece of paper is pressed onto the stone, and the ink is sucked up into its fibers. A different engraved stone is used for printing each color—as in the Lautrec posters.

The limitation of this process is that limestone isn't all that hard, and the edges of the ink-holding surfaces soon begin to break down, with the result that the printed lines lose their sharpness. A really fussy artist will use a stone for only forty prints. The maximum possible for an artist with any self-respect will fall somewhere between 150 and 200 prints.

By the middle 1800s lithographs were being made by etching zinc plates the same way because they would last for a few thousand impressions. Early circus posters, typically, were made with such zinc plates. In modern times the process of lithography has been adopted to high-speed printing by curving the engraved plates around a drum. The ink is rolled onto the drum, rolled off it onto a rubber roller, and then rolled from the rubber roller onto the paper—all so fast you can't see it happen.

Because of the porosity of the paper used, old lithographs cannot be retouched with oil-based paint—the paint will slowly seep beyond the area you want it in. But this will not occur if you use opaque water colors, which will dry before they have a chance to seep. These are called *gouache*, and they are sold in good art stores in a wide range of standard painters' colors. The usually preferred brand is Winsor and Newton's Designer's Gouache. The degree of flatness of the *gouaches* is the same as that of old lithograph ink—including that on the circus posters.

In the case of exceptionally porous paper, which has gotten much more absorbent than when it was originally imprinted, you can also run into trouble even with the opaque water colors. In that event the paper can be sized—either in the pertinent area or over the whole sheet. This is done with a very thin solution of colorless shellac (called "white," as opposed to the orange version). Make a solution of five parts of denatured alcohol to one part of shellac, and apply it with a camel's-hair brush.

A badly torn, deteriorated lithograph, as well as other prints on cheap, flaky paper (for instance, circus posters), can be "saved" by immersing it in a fifty-fifty solution of shellac and denatured alcohol. First you lay the poster out on a piece of backing paper of the same rusty-beige color. This backing sheet should be a couple of inches larger on all sides. You then lay the poster and backing sheet on a screen, which you lower into a large pan of the shellac solution. In about a minute you raise the screen, push the pieces of poster together the way they belong, and let everything dry for fifteen minutes while you wipe the excess shellac solution off the underside of the screen with paper towels so that the backing paper won't stick to the screen. If it does stick anywhere, a pad wetted with alcohol and rubbed on the bottom of the screen will loosen it even after the shellac has dried.

The treatment and possible removal of stains, mildew, foxing, flyspots, and all the other vicissitudes that can befall lithographs and anything else on paper are considered with faultless logic in the section on PAPER.

LOCKS

The commonest problem with locks isn't that they are broken but that they are working too darned well. Especially in the case of a locked drawer for which you have no key. But have no fear—help is here, for more ingenious minds than mine have been applied to this problem, and the solution to it is well-known among old-time cabinetmakers. Actually there are several solutions.

The best solution is based on the fact that locks are fastened to drawer fronts and cabinet doors from behind. So you attack from behind by taking the dust boards off the back of the case, which are always loosely fitted, anyway. Then you pry out the back of the drawer, and unscrew the screws that are holding the lock to the back of the drawer front. If you can't manage the screws, or if you run out of patience, you can pry the lock out with a screw driver. This means you will have to do a little restorative gluing later, but the important thing is that you won't have defaced the front of the drawer or hurt the lock.

If the drawer above your locked one can be removed, and there are not dust boards between the drawers, you are in real luck because you can reach in from above to get at the back of your lock, which you get to see by propping up a small mirror in the locked drawer.

Now you can take your lock to your local locksmith, who will probably be able to find the key that fits it by just glancing at the lock. Or in two minutes at the most. (Of course, with chests small enough to be carried, this is what you do in the first place.)

When getting to a lock from behind isn't worth the work involved, the standard procedure—especially with tiny locks on small drawers—is to push the lock back into the drawer. To do this you use a small rod—that just fills the swivel hole—to press against the swivel pin that you will see is in the center of the hole. Your rod can be a common nail with its point ground or filed flat, but large enough so that the swivel hole will hold it straight. A punch used for countersinking nails is excellent because of its indented point, which fits on the swivel pin.

Now you put your rod in the swivel hole and tap it sharply about twenty times. If this doesn't do the job, it will at least have loosened things up, and you start increasing the sharpness of your tapping until the lock does go backward.

In the case of a slant-front desk or a cupboard that is locked, there is, of course, a whole other approach: you undo the hinges. To do this, you just tap the swivel pins out of their hinges. Apply a little Liquid Wrench and tap patiently. Use a nail a little smaller than the pin—after you have filed the point off the nail, of course. The pins in cupboard hinges,

*Nail punch, or set, is used to drive in key pin
to remove drawer locks.*

naturally, are tapped up. Desk-front hinges come out either
way.

Cleaning a rusty lock is the next most popular problem. Almost all locks were iron until brass became popular around
the early 1700s for use in the English and French furniture of
that period—the Golden Century of furniture design.

To do the job right, the lock should be removed from any
wood onto which it is mounted—to avoid staining the wood
with the rust dissolvers. To loosen the screws holding the lock
together, either Liquid Wrench or Naval Jelly will work most
of the time. For a hard job use both, and in this way: First
soak the rust with applications of Liquid Wrench at two-hour
intervals all day, and let the piece set overnight. Then wash it
with mineral spirits, and heat it over a gas flame until all the
smoking stops—and for a couple of minutes more after that.
When the metal has cooled soak it with the Naval Jelly and
leave it overnight. To remove all the remaining gunk from
places you can't get at, boil the lock in a strong solution of
Spic and Span.

If any parts of the lock have been damaged—by a previous

forcible entry, for instance—before trying to bend them back into their original shape, or before doing whatever work has to be done, the metal should be softened. This is done by holding the piece or the whole lock over a gas flame until it begins to turn red. Full red won't hurt it, but it isn't necessary. Then you plunge it into a dishpan of cold water.

This process, called annealing, does make the metal a lot softer, and bent pieces of the lock's mechanism or case can be hammered back into shape. Of course, with really old, massive locks, it is safer to hammer the metal while it is still red, but this naturally involves a good pair of blacksmith's tongs and a heavy metal plate on which to work.

Cast-iron locks of the Victorian era cannot be worked on this way, but in any event, they didn't get bent in the first place—they broke.

After a lock has been restored, use no lubricant on it except powdered graphite, because graphite will not absorb dust the way any oil will.

To restore the old look to iron that has been cleaned by chemicals, annealing, or wire-brushing, you can use the bluing that is sold in sporting-goods stores for use on the rifle barrels. Then tone down the shine of the bluing finish by wiping it with a little raw umber straight from a tube of artist's oil paint. This will dry by itself in a few days in a warm place.

For related information about working with iron, see CAST IRON and GUNS. For soldering and brazing see JEWELRY. For working on brass locks, see BRASS and COPPER.

MARBLE

It is strange how many people tell you to take your troubles with marble to an expert when it is such a reasonable material to work with and to restore—whether it be dirty, dulled, stained, mildewed, or broken. I suppose the reason is that we all associate marble with the high art of ancient Greek statues, Michelangelo's "Pietà" and other fine works of art both religious and republican.

But everything made out of marble isn't great. In fact a good 90 per cent of things made out of marble are commonplace. As art, the best thing that can be said for them is that they are decorative. And I can't think of anything kind at all to be said of the use of white marble as a table top. The fellow that thought that up should have had his head examined for, in spite of all its virtues, marble is easily scratched or scuffed and sucks in stains as fast as unfinished wood will.

To begin at the beginning, the reason that the folks in Athens started using marble for sculpture wasn't that they happened to have a quarry full of it nearby. The reason was that marble has a unique characteristic. It is a rock that is translucent. Light penetrates its surface about a quarter of an inch and gives a sculpture of which it is made a life of its own. Protruding surfaces glow, and the glow changes, depending on where the light comes from. This is why there is all the difference in the world between a head carved out of marble and one cast in plaster of Paris. There are many kinds of marble, however, so don't get upset if some marble that you have doesn't do this. In fact, little of the marble you find on a Victorian table is very translucent. On the other hand, the only

marble that sculptors will take seriously is the most translucent stuff from the quarries in Carrara, Italy.

The variations in marble result from the fact that it is really limestone—a quite opaque sedimentary rock—that was
crystallized eons ago by heat and pressure inside the earth.
Depending on the amount of heat and pressure, each deposit
was crystallized to a different extent. Then, too, the presence
of various oxides in the limestone resulted in marble of many
colors—from pale pink to bright green streaks in solid black.
You obviously do not get translucence in dark marbles, but
they are valued because they can be cut and polished to a
glasslike surface. They are also harder than the white and so
are good in the lobbies of public buildings.

Which brings us to the second reason the Greeks chose
marble—it carves beautifully. Not only is it soft for a stone,
but it is even-grained and so doesn't frustrate the sculptor by
chipping or splitting. A furniture doctor might even call it the
mahogany of stones.

Marble's porosity didn't bother the Greeks, of course, because it never occurred to them to use it as table tops. But to
be fair, the Greeks knew only their fine marble. The American marble used on good Victorian furniture is an example of
a degree of crystallization halfway between really good marble
and plain old white limestone. It is all a matter of degree, and
I have seen dull white tops on Victorian furniture that were
unquestionably plain, ordinary, white limestone—that is, having no translucence whatsoever.

This nonmarble was also widely used in Victorian bar-
bershops and men's rooms, and so it is still commonly found
today in junkyards that carry used building materials. And
there are still plenty of Victorian office buildings—with a
washroom on each floor—that haven't been torn down. The
point is that slabs of this polished white limestone are quite

easily available and can be used for replacing lost or smashed pieces. Often fancy edges are carved on them—with grindstones and files; they are stained various colors; even the characteristic streaks are painted on them to simulate marble. This was also done frequently in the Victorian era, and so you can find not only fake marble but also *antique* fake marble.

Now, more or less in order of severity, these are the defects found in antique marble objects and the process followed in correcting them:

Cleaning

Marble—like limestone—reacts to all kinds of acids, and so the best general cleaning agents to use are those of the "spirits" family. However, if there is any gloss remaining on the surface, you start out with plain mild soap and water applied with a soft rag. If not—as in statuary left outdoors—go ahead and use a bristle brush. This is done first, because some dirt is soluble in water only. You can also use denatured alcohol mixed with an equal amount of water for this preliminary cleaning.

Out-of-doors statues are often cleaned only by spraying them with water from garden hoses for twenty-four to forty-eight hours. This is far more effective than rain, because the spray can be directed from the side at areas that rain doesn't hit directly. (You will notice that the tops of the heads of outdoor statues are always clean.) If spraying doesn't do the job, the spirits to be used are mineral spirits, carbon tetrachloride, and benzene. It is traditional to use a mixture of a gallon of carbon tetrachloride with a quart of benzene. Gasoline, acetone, lacquer thinner, and even ether are all perfectly safe to use.

Much stronger in its effect on the marble is ammonia, which will quickly react with the stone and destroy any gloss on the surface. Knowing this is going to happen, you would use ammonia only for spot cleaning of areas on which nothing else will work. You scrub the ammonia on full strength with a stiff brush—usually toothbrush—after you have masked or covered surrounding areas that might get splattered. Later the gloss on the surface so cleaned can be restored by buffing. (See *Polishing*, page 134.)

Stains

Although stains can occur on any marble—even on outdoor statues at a rowdy garden party—they naturally occur most often on table tops, and we will discuss them in that context. Stains fall into two categories, each demanding different treatments: water-borne and oily.

Typical water-borne stains are ink, grape juice, coffee, tea, water-color paint, or dye from a wet fabric or book cover. The porous marble may have sucked the coloring in as much as a sixty-fourth of an inch.

The first step is to dry the surface of the marble thoroughly so that it will be able to suck in our bleach. With small pieces this can be done in a warming oven or in any oven that can be set at around 150° F., which is common in good kitchen stoves. The piece should be left in the oven for twenty-four hours.

In the case of a table top or other piece too large for an oven, heat can be applied with radiant electric heaters or even by hot sunshine on a dry summer day. (Prolonged exposure to bright sunshine, even inside a window, will in itself remove some stains—just as it bleaches them out of fabrics.)

Now, the bleach to be used has the frightening name of

oxalic acid—and I know that I just said that acids should not be used on marble. But that was for cleaning, and stain removing demands sterner measures. You make a saturate solution by dissolving the oxalic-acid crystals (which you get at a paint and hardware store) in a quart bottle of warm water until they begin to pile up on the bottom of the jar because the water has become saturated with them.

You might want to use oxalic acid only on spots on a statue, so you contain it with dikes of modeling clay. But on a table top it is best to apply it to the whole surface so that the bleaching process will be evenly distributed and you won't end up with a "spot" of cleanness. Let this solution soak into the marble for eight to twelve hours. (Keep the surface evenly wet by covering it with rags onto which you pour the solution.) By that time most stains that can be bleached out this way will have been removed. However, the next step is to soak the marble in a tub of water or under running water from a garden hose for twenty-four hours, to remove more spots and definitely lighten some others.

After the piece has dried, traces of stain that wouldn't come out can be obscured by rubbing and smudging the surface with a piece of ordinary white chalk.

Oily stains on marble are an entirely different matter. These can be caused by butter, chocolate candy, dripping candle wax, and so forth, and for such stains there in no point in drying out the marble. Heating would only drive the oils in deeper. What you do instead is to apply a compress to soak the solvent into the marble for twenty-four hours.

Since we rarely know what a greasy or oily stain was caused by, it is hard to know which of the spirit solvents mentioned above is best for a given spot. But one that is certainly effective on them all is a fifty-fifty mixture of carbon tetrachloride and benzene. What comes to about the same thing is a fifty-

fifty mixture of unleaded gasoline and a fabric dry-cleaning fluid.

The compress is a layer of whiting covered with cloth. The whiting is powdered chalk, which you can buy at your hardware store in one-pound packages. First, cover the area to be treated with whiting to a depth of half an inch. Then cover that with a piece of old sheeting or towel so that you can pour your solvent on without dispersing the whiting. It is easier, in fact, if you stir a paste of the solvent and the whiting in a cup to start with. Also, you can keep your compress wet during the soaking period by putting a piece of plastic wrapping material over it.

At the end of the twenty-four-hour soaking period allow the compress to dry out. As this occurs, the compress dries first and then sucks the solvent back up out of the marble, bearing the oil or grease with it. If it doesn't work completely the first time, repeat the process as often as necessary, because each treatment will show a definite improvement.

Polishing

Not only the foregoing treatments, but a lot of other things, too, tend to break down the shiny surface of polished marble. Such as wear—as on a table top—weathering out of doors, and even small amounts of gases in the air. A lot of old marble pieces were dulled by being kept in buildings once illuminated by gas and kerosene lamps.

So, repolishing is often a desirable thing to do, even if laborious and time consuming. For instance, it will take the average newcomer to the process a good eight hours of rubbing to repolish a marble table top measuring, say, twenty by thirty inches. And that is the kind of hard rubbing that is best done for only about an hour or two a day. Or course, by using various machines designed specifically for the process, an experienced worker can do the job in a quarter of that time. At any rate, the process is simply one of grinding the surface with progressively finer abrasives.

In order of use, these are: powdered pumice; wet-and-dry paper, starting with grade 300, then 400, 500, and 600; finally, white-rouge buffing compound. A protective coating of white bowling alley wax is then usually applied. All these materials can be bought in a good hardware store.

The powdered pumice must first be made into a paste. About two pounds of it is enough for the average job, and this is stirred into a gallon of water in a large pot or pail. The pail is allowed to sit overnight while the pumice settles to the bottom. The top water is poured off, and the paste at the bottom of the pail is what you use.

You rub the paste onto the surface with flat blocks of hard wood. A handy size is about 3½" wide by 7" or 8" long and 1" thick. Hard woods such as oak or maple are best, but pine will do if you replace it when its flatness begins to wear off. There are also special blocks for this purpose faced with hard rubber—available through your local tombstone store.

As you rub the pumice onto the marble, keep wetting it with a little water as needed. It should be kept at the consistency of slurry, which is a slush or thin paste, and when it is at that consistency will feel the grinding take place. There is no way to say how long this should go on, because it depends on your strength, the roughness of the surface, and the hardness of the stone. Very approximately, it should take the average-sized man who is used to doing physical labor about two hours. The only exact criterion for the need of more rubbing is that the marble hasn't gotten any smoother, but this is hard for a newcomer to the trade to judge. On the other hand, you must not overdo it. Just play it safe, and keep rubbing until you are *sure* the surface is as smooth as it will get this way. If you are not all that strong these days, make it four hours. And you can do it at the rate of an hour a day—and even break that up into two half-hour periods.

Now the wet-and-dry paper. For the average table top you will need two sheets each of the four grades—300, 400, 500, and 600. This is emery paper, but it has to say "wet-and-dry" on it, because we want to use it wet. With water, of course. Starting with grade 300, cut each sheet in half and wrap a half around your piece of hard flat wood. Keep the surface of the marble wet by sprinkling water on with your fingers, and wear out your sheets of each grade before going on to the next one. This should take you approximately a half an hour of rubbing for each grade. But *be sure* to flush and wipe the marble clean between rubbing it with each grade of paper. Use a garden hose, and be sure you get all the grit of the previous grade of paper off the surface before you start using the next finest.

After you have finished with your 600-grade paper, flush and wipe again, of course, and you are ready for the final buffing with white rouge. This is a very, very, fine abrasive, which is the same as the jeweler's rouge used in silver polish except that it is white. It comes in a solid stick about an inch in diameter and four inches long. To get it, you will probably have to buy a set of such sticks in four different colors, which indicate their degree of fineness. White is the finest.

Obviously, you can apply the rouge by hand, using a soft cloth as you would for polishing silver. But I can't tell you how long it would take because nobody has done it that way since electric hand drills were invented. These can be fitted with small buffing wheels, and the one to use is only three inches in diameter. The surface of the larger ones is traveling too fast. The polishing bonnets that fit over sanding disks can also be used, but the buffing wheels are better, because you can apply more force. In fact, if you get deeply into polishing marble, you will want to buy a heavier drill and a rheostat to slow down its speed to 900 r.p.m. so that you can exert real pressure without burning the drill out.

The white rouge is applied to the buffer while it is spinning. You just push the end of the stick against the spinning cloth, and the rouge rubs off onto it. Then you rub the buffer from side to side against the marble. There is no trouble deciding how long you have to do this because, with the kind of thrill everybody should experience at least once in his life, you will see the surface getting glossy.

Wipe the whole surface with a damp rag once in a while to see if there are any dull spots you have missed. When you are done, give the surface a waxing the same way you would a varnished table top—just for protection under normal use.

Grinding

Marble can be drilled, sawed, chiseled, filed, ground, and a few other things. Of course, it can't be shaped to your will as fast as wood can, but once you get used to the slower pace, you begin to realize that you can do anything with it that you can do with wood. And just as with wood, it is slower if you are using hand tools instead of specially designed power tools.

For instance, you can get a marble-cutting saw to put in your table saw. And routers with which to grind curbed edges. But working marble is called grinding because the tool that does most of the work is the grindstone. For roughing out, you use three-inch stones of various fineness that can be driven by your quarter-inch electric hand drill. For the finishing work you can use fine little grinders and sanding disks that come with Dremel's Moto-Tool; this is essentially a small electric drill that fits in the palm of your hand and is available at hobby shops and hardware stores.

With these machines, broken edges can be recarved to eliminate chips or places where small pieces have been broken off the edge of a table top. Polishing such "repairs" is done in the same way as described above, the blocks of wood carved to fit into or over curved surfaces.

Broken Pieces

Gluing two pieces of marble back together has suddenly become easier than it has been in the last three thousand years because of the advent of the self-setting epoxy glues. These are especially good for use with marble because they allow the light to continue to flow through the translucent surface of the stone.

The process is so similar to that for repairing china and porcelain that there isn't anything special to say about it here. So see CERAMICS.

Missing Pieces

Again, the techniques of filling holes and replacing missing parts in marble is so similar to those for repairing chinaware that there is no point in repeating them here. Except that for repairing marble you can buy marble dust to mix into the epoxy glue to form a patching putty. And if you mix this thinly—that is, with no more of the dust than is necessary— you can even get a translucence that matches the marble's.

Because regular epoxy is such a runny mixture, for this work you should use one of the "five-minute" epoxy glues and shape the material as it begins to harden, later sanding it smooth and glazing it with a thin coat of epoxy. But first read CERAMICS.

Protection

If it is to be kept indoors, marble is best protected by waxing it with a colorless paste furniture wax. You dust, clean, and rewax it as it becomes necessary, the same way you would take care of a fine piece of furniture. But for a piece of marble that is doomed to live outdoors, you want a tougher wax, and the more beeswax you use in any wax formula the tougher the formula will be. The easiest way to get such a wax is to melt your paste wax and add to it about 25 per cent beeswax—slivered to melt more easily into the liquid paste wax.

After this mixture has cooled, you wipe it on, but let it dry for a couple of days before you buff it. Otherwise it will be too gummy. For more on outdoor statuary see LIMESTONE. In fact, for related information concerning all problems with marble, see both LIMESTONE and ALABASTER.

MIRRORS

In many places in this book we have come up against the question of how much restoration should be done to an antique—or whether any restoration at all should be done. Is dust in the crevices of a gilded carving antique dust, or is it just dirt? Is rust on an antique gun antique and meaningful, or shouldn't the gun be returned as nearly as possible to its original condition? And doesn't that depend on whether the rust was acquired long ago or recently?

But there seems to be no disagreement at all on the subject of resilvering an antique mirror. The answer is no. It is never desirable or permissible for any reason whatsoever. Anyone committing this act or allowing or causing it to be done is a Hun, a Visigoth, a Barbarian, a cretin.

However, if I may interject a personal note here, I have now spent most of my life finding out how things are done in all the crafts relating to antiques: how things are made, how they are restored—and even faked to deceive the unwary. This has mostly involved asking questions of practicing craftsmen. And I have traveled all over this country and even some of Europe to find them.

But I have also looked at every book on crafts that I could find. And over and over in these I have read the most frustrating words (for me) "ever writ by pen." And these are not, "it might have been" but, "this problem should be placed in the hands of an expert." It was exactly what the expert knows that I was trying to find out.

I have pledged myself never to do that in this book, and so I am forced to tell you how to resilver a mirror even though I abhor the thought of anyone doing it. Begging your forgiveness, I shall explain what you are not supposed to do.

The process is not as hard as you might expect. What is hard is getting the material, for what you need to make eight ounces of silvering solution is one-eighth of an ounce of pure silver-nitrate crystals, which you can obtain only through a chemical-supply house catering to professional chemists, jewelry manufacturers, and, of course, mirror makers.

The silver-nitrate crystals are dissolved in eight ounces of distilled water with the aid of three drops of pure (26 degree) ammonia. This is poured on the back of the glass, which lies in a shallow pan, until the silver precipitates onto the glass. As a rule, it is best to leave the glass sitting in the solution overnight.

Now, several things remain to be said. Silver nitrate is a very strong acid that will react with almost anything except glass. For this reason it is mixed in the distilled water in a glass jar and stirred *only* with a glass rod. The pan in which the mirror glass rests must also be of glass or enamelware (which is glass).

The second thing is that your success in the process rests entirely on absolute scientific cleanliness. That applies to the inside of the mixing jar, the glass stirring rod, the glass to be silvered, and the pan in which it rests. This is achieved by cleaning them all with detergent, polishing them well with silver polish, removing every trace of the polish, and then cleaning all the surfaces with a 5 per cent solution of the pure ammonia in more distilled water. Then you rinse them with another quart of distilled water, letting them drip-dry. For the whole process you will need a gallon of distilled water.

After the glass has rested in the nitric acid solution over-night, you remove it—handling it by the edges with rubber gloves, of course—and stand it on edge, letting it drain by it-self and dry for an hour in warm dry air. Then you spray a protective coating of flat black lacquer onto it. Otherwise you would have a "see through" mirror or "one-way glass."

MUSIC BOXES

Any music box made so long ago as to be called an antique will have been so carefully and soundly made that it will never wear out. Built-in-obsolescence had yet to be thought of, and people made things to last forever—or at least a cou-ple of thousand years. However, dirt and rust can cause a music box mechanism to slow down, and once in a thousand times a spring will have broken. Much more likely, the spring will have become detached inside its containing barrel.

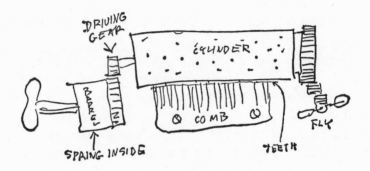

Anatomy of a music box.

First, a few definitions are in order.

On one end of the brass *cylinder* with the tiny *pins* sticking out of it is the *barrel* that contains the *spring* that moves the *driving gear* that makes the cylinder revolve, causing the pins to hit the *teeth* of the steel *comb* which vibrate to create the musical notes.

On the other end of the cylinder you will find a *regulating gear* attached to the cylinder. This gear connects to a set of smaller gears that drive a *fly*; because the vanes of the fly spin around only so fast in the air, they retard the speed with which the drum can revolve and cause the cylinder to revolve at a constant speed. Because the air is thinner in Denver or Mexico City, a music box will play faster there than it will in a city at sea level. Of course, this can be corrected by enlarging the vanes slightly.

The first step in cleaning or repairing one of the *movements* is to unscrew the *bedplate* on which the whole mechanism is mounted from the wood to which it is attached by said screws. Now that you can get at it, a general washing can be given with Liquid Wrench, applied with small bristle brushes that artists use for oil painting. Then you oil the bearings—but *never* the teeth of the gears—with watch oil that you obtain from your local jeweler.

The bearings of the fly are the most important, and there will probably be a screw enabling you to take out the fly so that you can clean its bearings with a pin point.

If the comb is rusty, you will note that this, too, can be unscrewed so that you can get at its underside to give it a proper cleaning with Liquid Wrench and Naval Jelly if necessary. In doing this, use only bristle brushes or the sharpened ends of flat toothpicks while the teeth are supported by the flat surface of a block of wood. This will make it harder for you to break, bend, or scratch the teeth.

In the case of a detached or broken spring, you will note that there are various screws that will release the cylinder so as to disengage its power-receiving gear from the driving gear. Then you can remove the barrel. More screws will enable you to open it to inspect the spring. If this is detached, it will be a simple matter to slip the hole in the end of it over the retaining lug.

If the spring is broken or badly rusted, take it to a watchmaker (employed by a large jewelry store), who will have a catalogue from which he can order a replacement. The replacement does not have to be exactly the same size. It just can't be any bigger. But it doesn't matter if it is slightly thinner or shorter, because it is not the power of the spring that controls the speed at which the cylinder revolves, but the fly.

For replacing a totally ruined or lost movement, you can buy a new one. Movements range from ones playing only one tune with eighteen notes to ones playing six tunes on forty-one notes. To inquire about the tunes available write a nice letter to Albert Constantine & Son, Inc., 2050 Eastchester Road, New York, New York 10461.

OIL PAINTINGS

The trouble with oil paintings is the primer that artists put on the canvas to make it smoother and nonabsorbent. This primer, which is called gesso, consists of an animal glue into which some powdered gypsum has been worked. The result amounts to having applied a thin coat of plaster of Paris to the canvas. Gypsum is a mineral deposit that when powdered and dried out *is* plaster of Paris. It is so called because it was prepared from the deposits of gypsum near the city of Paris in the area now known as Montmartre.

The trouble comes when too much moisture gets into the gesso. Changes of heat—just from summer to winter—then cause the layer of paint and the gesso to expand and contract at different rates. While this movement may be infinitesimal, we are talking about its happening once a year over a century or three or four.

Now, all this is quite pertinent to how oil paintings are cleaned and restored, for the different rates of expansion and contraction in the layers of a painting are what cause cracking, bulging, cupping, and flaking. The basic treatment of a decaying oil painting is to remove the canvas from the back of the painting and replace it with new canvas that is glued on with beeswax hardened with a little resin.

This is not as incredible an operation as it sounds once you know how it is done, although, admittedly, it has to be done with care and patience. The term for it is "lining," and it has been done—several times in many cases—to great masterpieces: certainly to almost all the great Flemish and Dutch

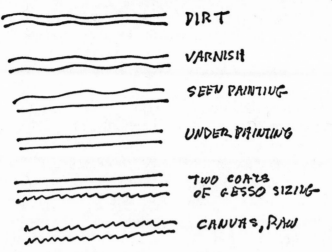

Cross section of an oil painting.

paintings—even to Rembrandt's giant painting "Night Watch."

Any craft-oriented person can learn to do it and get miraculous results—although I assume you will get some practice first on paintings of less value than your Rembrandts. I call the results miraculous, because a flaky, cracked painting obviously cannot simply be cleaned without destroying it. After lining, however, the surface is so stabilized that it can be cleaned very satisfactorily—even when the varnish (shellac) on the surface of the oil paint was so impregnated with soot that you couldn't see the image.

So far, I have been talking about paintings that are in extreme conditions of decay. Some old paintings are in good enough condition that all they need is cleaning, and this can be done without lining. Some cracking can be corrected with heat and weights. Tears and holes can be patched with spot lining and retouching. So I will begin with the process of cleaning and work up the scale of difficulty with bulges, cracking, cupping, and flaking, patching holes and tears, and finally lining. I will end up with retouching and revarnishing.

Cleaning

Since the earliest days of oil painting, it has been the practice to protect a painting with a protective coat of shellac, or "spirit varnish," as opposed to the linseed oil cum resin varnishes. The process of cleaning an oil painting, then, involves cleaning the surface dirt off the shellac first and then removing the shellac into which the grime and dirt has worked itself.

The surface dirt is removed with turpentine or mineral spirits. This can be applied and wiped up with soft brushes or cotton. If this is all the cleaning to be done, paste furniture wax is excellent because of its high content of mineral spirits; as you wipe it off, it leaves a thin coat of wax on the varnish, which not only prevents dust from getting into the shellac but clarifies the colors of the painting.

Soap and water are not used, or even water alone, because there may be microscopic cracks in the painting through which the water can get at the gesso to cause the cracks to worsen.

To remove the shellac—or at least all but a thin film of it—denatured alcohol is the basic solvent to use. It must be from a fresh, sealed can to be sure it hasn't absorbed any water from the air as, being highly anhydrous, it does very rapidly.

Given a shellac that dissolves easily and paint underneath it of the best quality that has thoroughly hardened, the alcohol can be applied full-strength with a brush to a small area at a time and picked up with cotton balls or Q-tips. To find out if this is going to be possible, try it out on tiny test areas. However, ideal conditions being as rare in old paintings as they are in everything else, the standard practice is to use a solution of half alcohol and half turpentine.

Castor oil, although it is an ingredient of some patented oil painting cleaners, should not be used—simply because nothing should be used that will not fully evaporate in the event that it gets into the gesso through a crack. No water, no oil— just volatile spirits.

The use of turpentine with alcohol prevents the appearance of a white bloom on the oil painting in case all the shellac has come off. Some shellac should be left, however, and it is not difficult to remove shellac in such a way as to leave a trace of it on the surface. To have taken up this trace, you would have to have been wiping harder than you were supposed to be doing in the first place.

If any traces of paint begin to come off onto your cotton balls or Q-tips, you have run into a paint of inferior quality— usually one in which white lead or bitumen was used. All you can do is stop—unless it is just one color that is coming off, and then you can work around it.

If the shellac does not come out of pitted places or valleys caused by the original brush strokes, the first thing to do is increase the time you have been letting the alcohol-turpentine mixture stand on the surface to soften the shellac. Keep the surface wet for three to six times as long before picking up the shellac with a camel's-hair brush. Always try out any change in procedure on a small test area first, of course.

If you still can't get this dirty shellac out of crevices in the oil paint, you can try the technique that museum restorers use on a masterpiece—scratch it out with a surgeon's scalpel. Museum restorers work with a ten-power magnifying glass and reconcile themselves to cleaning about half a square inch a day. Just how close to this standard you want to get is a value judgment you alone can make.

After it is cleaned, the painting is allowed to dry for twenty-four hours, and a new coat of shellac is applied with a wide camel's-hair brush. You must use fresh shellac, thinned 25 per cent with denatured alcohol, and apply it in a dry atmosphere to avoid bloom. After forty-eight hours give it a second coat. The reason for this thick coating is to make it easier for the restorer who will be cleaning it again in the future. Shellac is used instead of any modern lacquer for the same reason. It is the softest and most removable clear coating you can use.

To help that future restorer even more, after the second coat of shellac has dried for a week or two it should be waxed with a paste furniture wax to help keep dust and grime out of the shellac.

Bulging

Sometimes the only harm that moisture has caused is an uneven surface called bulging. To cure this, the canvas must be taken off the stretcher and pressed flat.

To protect the surface of the painting, it is placed face down on a perfectly flat surface (masonite) that has been covered with a single layer of a thin woolen blanket. But sheets of waxed paper must separate the face of the painting from the wool. Then a piece of masonite or prestwood is cut to just cover the back of the painting, and a lot of weight is piled on. Concrete blocks are the best thing—three layers.

Clamps can be used, but they involve two pieces of three-quarter-inch plywood cut to the size of the painting, leaving the tacking edges hanging out. You will also cut a piece of woolen blanket the size of the plywood pieces and use it to cushion the face. And don't forget the waxed paper. The boards are then squeezed together with wooden clamps or C-clamps.

The clamp method—or the concrete block method—should work in a week to a month. If results are slow—or too slow for *you*—you can heat the boards by standing them in a sunny window, changing sides daily, or put them over a radiator or heat them with an electric heat projector.

Cracking

If cracking has occurred only in the "varnish," it is simply removed by the method discussed above in *Cleaning*. But if the cracks occur in the paint, they are caused by cracking of the gesso beneath. And the next steps in deterioration will be cupping and flaking of the little islands of paint caused by the cracking.

But, first, simple cracking: The problem that this presents is that, in the cleaning of the painting, dirty shellac will get into the cracks, creating a network of fine, dark lines. The first step in preventing this is to remove the canvas from its stretcher and, suitably protecting its face with wax paper and a cushion, to iron it from behind with an electric clothes iron set at warm. This will close the cracks considerably. Some of the paraffin on the paper might fill them, which is all to the good, as this will help to keep dirt out of them. Peel the waxed paper off while the painting is still warm.

The second thing you can do to keep dirt from getting into the cracks is to clean the painting by rolling the alcohol-and-turpentine solvent on the surface with cotton balls that have been wetted with it and then squeezed half dry. This is followed by rolling with dry balls of cotton. No wiping, no scrubbing—just rolling.

Only after having removed 95 per cent of the shellac may you try brushing the cracks clean with a camel's-hair brush dipped in the solvent.

A fresh coat of shellac is then applied as discussed above

under *Cleaning*. To protect such a painting from behind, it should first be dried out in a warm, dry room for a few days to a week, and then the back can be sealed from moisture with a heavy coat of shellac or the beeswax-resin mixture used for lining.

Cupping

On the road to total disintegration, halfway between cracking and flaking, we find cupping. The little islands of paint caused by cracking have begun to turn up at the edges.

Once a painting has deteriorated to the cupping stage, the canvas and gesso are most likely to be in such bad shape that lining is necessary. This becomes a matter of judgment as to whether the painting is worth the effort. And don't feel that you are alone in this because such decisions are constantly being mulled over in the back rooms of museums the world over.

Cupping can be brought somewhat under control, however. The first step is to flatten the painting with pressure, as discussed under *Bulging*, and then to iron the painting, as discussed under *Cracking*.

The second step is to stabilize the painting by coating the front of it with shellac and the back of it with a beeswax-resin mixture.

Flaking

Flaking is a condition that fills me with quotations from Hippocrates. Like "Extreme conditions demand extreme remedies" and "Life is short, art is long; the conditions mysterious; decision difficult; experiment perilous."

The best that can be done is to spray the surface with a

mist of clear lacquer by pointing the spray above the surface and letting the mist settle until the surface is thoroughly wet. As soon as the lacquer has set but not thoroughly dried, press down any curly flakes with your fingertip. Keep spraying on additional coats of lacquer until you have built up a solid film. This can be covered with shellac for future cleaning. At any rate, with the flakes established in a film, lining can then be done.

Patching

The process of patching holes and tears is so similar to lining that a natural question comes up: If a piece is worth patching, why isn't it worth doing a good job and lining the whole painting? For all that patching amounts to is mounting new canvas on the back of the damaged area the same way you mount it on the whole back of the painting in lining.

The only important difference is that you feather the edges of your patch so that they can't show on the front of the painting in case you iron your patch on too hard. And since that is all you need to know about the difference between patching and lining, we will proceed to lining.

Lining

Lining is the process of putting a new canvas support on the back of an oil painting. There are two very different degrees of lining, which we can call simple lining and extreme lining.

In simple lining all that happens is that you attach a new canvas to the back of the old one, both being impregnated, by warm ironing, with a tough mixture of beeswax and resin. In extreme lining the old canvas is removed from the back of the

gesso by sanding and scraping, and a new canvas is applied
with the beeswax-resin adhesive, which is a cute trick indeed.

Before we proceed with the step-by-step discussion of these
processes, I'm sure I can hear many voices murmuring, "But
why does he use such an old-fashioned adhesive as beeswax?
Now that we have really good glues like polyvinyl acetate
(white glue) or an epoxy, why not use them? And how about
a Fiberglas lining instead of canvas? Or gluing the painting to
masonite?"

Well, the answer is, when you think about it, that every
process you use in restoring a work of art should be reversible
—in consideration of the next restorer who will have to work
on it maybe next week or maybe a hundred or five hundred or
a thousand years from now. And by using a *thermoplastic*
"glue" we assure this reversibility. Obviously, the use of modern glues and board are going to make it much harder if not
impossible ever again to work on a painting from behind. At
least that is the way the people who care for historic paintings
and other antiques and works of art have been thinking for
the last few hundred years. And those who are doing it today
are not the kind of people who rush to accept change.

Should the "Mona Lisa" be suspended forever in a four-
inch-thick slab of lucite? It could certainly be done. But are
we absolutely certain that the lucite (or epoxy) won't turn
green in a thousand years? Or what if our taste in such matters changes in only a hundred years, as it already has with
many people, and we decide to paint her eyebrows and
eyelashes back on? You knew they had fallen off, didn't you,
and that the restorers who guard her have decided it would be
a sacrilege to retouch them?

So the principle of reversibility is hard to put down. In fact,
some experiments with change have already proved to be mistakes. Some paintings glued to board with an early version of

casein glue have begun to split and bulge, and nobody can think of a way that is worth the labor of getting them off the board to work on them.

If you want to break a little ground, however, there is one modern material that *is* finding acceptance, and that is using glass cloth instead of canvas. Since this is still used with the beeswax-resin adhesive, it doesn't go against the principle of reversibility. So in the following paragraphs you may read "glass cloth" for "canvas" if you wish.

Simple Lining

In simple lining, the painting is first taken off its stretcher and the edges that were tacked to the sides of the stretcher are trimmed off. By the time a painting needs lining, the edges will have frayed and decayed to such an extent that you won't be able to use them again, and so they are replaced by cutting the sheet of lining canvas an inch larger than the actual painting on all sides. Or you can leave two inches of extra canvas all around for easier handling and trim it down when you are ready to remount the canvas on its old stretcher, if possible, or a new one if necessary because of the old one's having rotted.

The painting is placed face down on a flat surface covered with a layer of woolen blanket, and the old canvas backing is prepared for the adhesive by scuffing it with sandpaper and then brushing and blowing the dust away. Then the new canvas is cut to size—which is oversize to provide new tacking edges, of course. This canvas should be the best linen canvas; it comes unsized in rolls at art-supply stores catering to professional artists. Most artists prefer to stretch and size their own canvases because raw, rolled canvas is much stronger than that used in the stretched and primed ones.

The adhesive is prepared by melting together the following:

Beeswax   16 ounces
Resin   12 ounces
Paraffin   4 ounces
Turpentine   3 ounces

This is, of course, a general-purpose formula. For a harder surface, you can use more resin in proportion to the beeswax. For more pliability, increase the amount of paraffin in proportion to the resin. So long as you stay somewhere near the basic formula, such changes aren't crucial to the effectiveness of the adhesive. They just change its character.

The heating of the waxes and the resin can be done in a double boiler. The heating is speeded if you start them already warm from sitting in a warming oven or on a radiator in the winter. The turpentine is added last.

Keeping the double boiler at a bare simmer, you apply coats of the wax with an ordinary paint brush to both the old canvas and one side of the new piece.

The two waxed surfaces are then joined, the waxed side of the new canvas being placed over the waxed surface of the old canvas. Then the new canvas is ironed with a clothes iron set at warm and with enough pressure so that the wax will not only come up through the new canvas but will also ooze into any imperfections in the old canvas and any cracks in the gesso or in the actual painting. This penetration by the wax is desirable for stabilizing the painting, and any excess that goes through to the face of the painting is easily removed by melting it with a warm, dull knife blade and then wiping it up with cotton.

The canvas is now trimmed and remounted on its original stretcher or on a new one. Then it can be cleaned, for when a painting is going to be lined, cleaning is left until after the lining has been applied. It makes the job easier and safer to have the paint surface as flat and stable as possible.

Extreme Lining

Until they know how it is done, most people are amazed that you can actually replace the old canvas of an oil painting. The trick is that first you stabilize the face of the painting by pasting alternate layers of cotton sheeting and newspaper to it with a simple flour and water paste.

Of course the whole painting must be pressed and/or ironed flat. Then start with a layer of cotton. First brush the paste onto the face of the painting. Lay the cotton on it, and brush some more paste onto it to make sure there are no air bubbles between the paint and the cotton. Lay a sheet of newspaper on the cotton and brush that down. (Paper towels can be used instead of newspaper.) Let this dry overnight and in the same way paste on another layer of cotton and one of paper. Let it dry overnight—or thoroughly—and repeat the process until you have built up a body of this cotton-reinforced cardboard about a quarter of an inch thick.

Now you are ready to scrape the old canvas off the back of the painting—in other words, off the gesso. This scraping must be done carefully. The best tool is a curved Exacto blade, but any very sharp curved blade will do. This is time consuming but neither difficult nor dangerous, for the rotten fibers of the canvas come off easily. Any fibers that are imbedded in the gesso, you just leave there. Or you use a brass brush of the kind used on suede shoes to remove the canvas fibers from the gesso if the brush is strong enough.

New canvas is now "glued" to the gesso in the same manner as described under *Simple Lining*. A second layer of canvas may be added in the same way.

To remove the "cast" you have placed on the face of the picture, you wet it with a sponge and peel off the top layer of cotton sheeting. Then you wet the surface again and peel off another layer until you come to the final one, which you make sure is completely softened by the water, and peel it off very carefully.

If this process seems a contradiction to the principle that water should never be applied to an oil painting, there are two arguments for breaking the rule. The first is that any cracks or porous places in the gesso should now be impregnated with beeswax, which will keep the water out of it. The second is that the museum persons who do this sort of thing for a living say that it is the best way they have yet found. At least the best way that is reversible.

Inpainting

Once a canvas has been lined and cleaned, any holes or tears in it are ready to be touched up or repainted. The purist's view of this matter is that the area should be colored evenly in only one shade approximating the colors around it. In other words, while the repaired area should not stand out, it should be completely obvious on close inspection.

On the other hand, straightforward repainting to blend in with the surrounding areas has been done over the centuries to at least half of the really old masterpieces, and that is still the method that is certainly used on any paintings restored commercially—that is, outside museums.

Whichever method is chosen, the technique is first to trim any loose fibers from the edges of the hole and then carefully feather the edges with fine sandpaper so that they will not appear as lines later on. Any wax left from lining is scraped out of the hole, and the hole is refilled with gesso to bring the surface level with the adjoining surface of the oil paint. Before

the gesso has completely dried, its surface is modeled to conform with the texture of the surrounding paint. This often involves pressing a piece of canvas on the half-dried gesso to
give it a corresponding weave texture.

The gesso is then varnished with picture varnish to prevent
it from dulling the paint by sucking it dry. Next, the
matching oil paints are applied, preferably by someone who
understands how to use oil paints. The point is that the
aliveness of oil paintings is a result of the different colors
being blended by the brush as they are applied. And you
don't learn much about this skill with a painting-by-the-
numbers kit.

Revarnishing

Oil paints dry slowly, and so this retouching should be allowed to dry in a nice dry room for about six months before
you revarnish the whole painting. If the varnish—shellac, that
is—is applied before the paint is thoroughly dry, it is likely to
"crawl," producing cracks. (As this implies, no new oil painting should be shellacked until it has dried for six months either.) Drying can, of course, be hastened by applying heat
one way or another—including the sun—but the surface temperature of the paint shouldn't go over 110° F. for more than
that could cause the paint to crack from internal stress.

When the shellac is applied, it should be taken from an
unopened jar or can. So should the denatured alcohol used to
thin it by about 15 per cent. This is because both are
anhydrous and quickly absorb moisture from the air, which
causes the shellac to "bloom"—to become foggy white in varying degrees. Also to avoid blooming, the shellac must be applied in a warm, dry room and allowed to dry thoroughly in
those conditions.

Bloom can be removed from a painting simply by brushing

the surface with fresh alcohol. This makes the bloom disappear immediately, but the surface must be allowed to dry out again in dry conditions. A coating of paste furniture wax over the shellac will prevent blooming in the future.

Wooden Panels

The typical oil painting on wood is of a religious nature and is four or five hundred years old—or well over that—and the problem is that the wood is worm-eaten or has been attacked by bacteria and fungus and so is powdering away.

The treatment for stopping further decay is to soak the wood in thymol dissolved in denatured alcohol (from your pharmacy). This can be brushed on freely with a soft brush, or the panel can be lowered face up in a pan of it, and after it has floated until the wood is saturated completely, it can be pushed down for full immersion for five seconds. Then set the panel on edge to drain.

In the case of extreme fragility, the panel can be treated with the fumes of thymol dissolved in a solution of half alcohol and half ether (instead of alcohol alone, which is the usual procedure). To do this, you suspend the panel in an airtight box and pour the thymol solution into a pan beneath the panel. This solution, which can be ordered for you by your pharmacist, can be poured—but quickly, and don't breathe any. As to the quantity, let the pan have half the area of the panel, and fill it a quarter-inch deep. And close the box quickly.

Some oil paintings on terribly decayed wood have actually been transferred to canvas by the method outlined in *Extreme Lining*.

PAPER

Much can be done for old prints, etchings, engravings and any other printed matter, because from the very beginnings of all printing processes the inks used have been very stable. With only rare exceptions they consist of various mixtures of linseed oil, pine resin, and carbon or lamp black. As a result they remain unaffected while we clean and bleach the paper with various water-based solutions.

The chief trouble that occurs with the paper is that it is very susceptible to mildew and the small specks of mildew called foxing. These conditions are actually caused by a fungus growth of bacteria that are dormant in dry conditions but grow with wild abandon in warm, moist air. They do not really grow in the fibers of the paper but feed on the size with which the paper has been treated to make it less absorbent and to stiffen it. This size was a gelatin or glue obtained by boiling animal hooves and hides.

Of course, there are other problems such as stains caused by oil, waxy substances, ink, dyes, colors in vegetable matter, flyspots, and physical damage caused by folding and tearing. For all these ills there are remedies of varying effectiveness. But to begin at the beginning . . .

Surface Dirt

Discoloring that often looks as if it is imbedded in the paper is often only on the surface; in any event, surface cleaning should be done before any other process is undertaken, lest you just be pushing dirt into the paper.

Dust should be brushed off with a soft paint brush or varnish brush. The next obvious thought is an eraser, but not the kind you find on the end of a pencil, for this will abrade the surface of the paper, and in precious documents or fine etchings, collectors will examine the surface against the light for just such "faults."

The best cleaner-eraser for paper is still the first one ever used: a wad of soft, moist bread. It doesn't have to be homemade bread either. Any of the cheap, spongy white breads that you buy at the supermarket will do. They are usually nice and soggy when fresh, and you knead the center of eight or so slices into a ball, which you *roll* hard on the paper. You can sprinkle water on the slices before wadding them to make them moister, and you just experiment to get the most effective degree of sogginess.

You can also buy a "kneaded eraser" in an art-supply store. This is a gummy, stretchable, kneadable rubber, which also picks up dirt when you press it onto or roll it over the surface of paper. But do not rub with it because there is some abrasive in it.

A more advanced general cleaning technique is actually to wash the paper in luke-warm water. This is done only when absolutely necessary, because it is almost certain to destroy the reflective quality of the size on the surface of the paper. This can be restored, however. (See below.)

The washing process is done by running mildly warm water through a photographic tray for three or four hours. Some paper can be washed for days with continuing improvement. You just have to keep checking frequently to see if any deterioration of the fiber structure is taking place. Soap or other solvent is never used—for grease stains see *Grease Spots*, below.

As to restoring a sized look to the surface of the paper, a gentle ironing is the first step—although ironing paper is in all other cases considered a destructive act. In Holland, for instance, the ironing of an original Rembrandt etching is punishable by life imprisonment, not to mention the fact that you have cut its value by about 85 per cent.

However, when resizing is considered appropriate—as on a poster that was heavily sized originally—the first ironing is followed by spraying a thin mist of lacquer on the paper. When this is dry you iron it into the surface. The iron, of course, should be only warm and coated with a silicone-based furniture polish. Repeated sprays of lacquer are applied until the amount of size satisfies you.

Obviously, this is a very delicate process and should not be attempted until you have gained considerable experience on many different kinds of paper, using expendable pieces and scrap.

I have told how it is done—the necessary judgment has to be acquired by you. When I say I have told how it is done, I mean only that I have told how it is generally done commercially. Purists have two other substances they use instead of the lacquer spray. These are washes of animal glue and *Knox* gelatin. But they both are more difficult substances to use than the lacquer spray, and as far as permanence goes, neither of them is as good.

Flyspots

Flyspots, or flyspecks, are deposits left by flies or other insects on the surface of paper. If this is what your spots really are, you can feel them with your fingertip.

So far, the only technique that has been developed for removing them is to pick them off with a needle and to bleach out the remaining stain with hydrogen peroxide, which is applied to just the stain area with a fine-pointed brush. Clorox may also be tried alternately with the peroxide for a stronger bleaching effect than either gives when it is used alone. Sometimes. It depends on the nature of the paper and what the fly had for lunch that day.

Both the picking with a needle and the bleaching are best done with a self-supporting magnifying glass or a 3X-power jeweler's loupe. Either is available through the mail-order catalogue of the Brookstone Company, Peterborough, New Hampshire 03458. Afterward the area can be burnished and sized as described above.

Mildew

Alternate terms for spreading mildew are fungus and mold; when mildew appears in spots similar to flyspots it is called foxing. The difference is that flyspots are black and can be felt on the surface of the paper. Foxing spots are brown and *in* the paper. Both the spreading and foxing kinds of mildew are caused by spores that under moist-enough conditions come to life and feed on the size in the paper, which is usually animal glue or starch. The spores may have been airborne to the paper or were dormant in the size and came to life when the paper got moist and warm enough.

Four bleaches are known to have the effect of lightening or totally eliminating the brown stains of mildew. The first is thymol, which is also an excellent disinfectant and will prevent future mold growth. It is a pharmaceutical product. It may be applied with a brush to the back of the paper, which has been placed face down on a flat surface covered with several layers of old cotton sheet or large white blotters obtainable at photographic-supply stores. You apply just enough to saturate the paper and keep it wet for an hour. No rinsing is necessary for it evaporates rapidly. Containing no water and being an alcoholic solution, it will not cause the paper to deteriorate.

The only trouble is that thymol doesn't always work because there are so many kinds of size and mildew-causing fungi. In that event, you can try hydrogen peroxide of the strength sold in drugstores. This can also be brushed on the back—or with a wide camel's-hair brush even on the front of the paper.

But very fragile pieces of paper should be exposed only to the fumes of hydrogen peroxide. This is done by pouring a thin mixture of plaster of Paris into a shallow tray to the depth of half an inch. When this has set and dried out for a week in a warm spot, you pour the hydrogen peroxide on it until it won't absorb any more. Then you suspend the face of the paper over this fuming surface. The simple way to do this is to lay a sheet of plastic window screening right on the fuming surface and the paper face down on top of that. Or the paper can be held between two tightly stretched pieces of plastic screening for placing over the plaster slab. For best results, the whole operation can be covered with an airtight cover to contain the fumes for several hours, but you may get perfectly adequate results without going to that extent.

A third bleach to try is a solution of one rounded tablespoonful of oxalic-acid crystals (from a paint or drugstore) in a quart of warm water. Your paper has to be floated face down on this until it is wetted through. Only a minute or two will do it. Whatever it is going to do, oxalic acid does it fast or not at all. The paper must then be gently rinsed in room-temperature running water for five minutes. Needless to say, this treatment is not recommended for very delicate paper.

The fourth bleach that can be used is a thin solution of Clorox—a half cup to a quart of water. You can experiment with making the mixture stronger. However, this bleach is very likely to turn the whole sheet of paper a startling white. In this event, after rinsing the Clorox out for five minutes and letting it dry thoroughly, dip it in some black coffee or a stain made by boiling up some chewing tobacco. You won't be the first one to have done it.

Grease Spots

For removing greasy or oily spots, get some large white blotters used for drying photographic prints from any good-sized photographic-supply store. Cut two pieces of the blotter —they are really large—half an inch larger all around than the paper you want to clean. Dampen these with carbon tetrachloride, which is a nonflammable cleaning fluid, and press your paper between them with a medium-warm iron.

Alternately, you can wet your paper with the carbon tetrachloride and press it between two pieces of dry blotter.

If these treatments do not work completely, switch to benzene or mineral spirits. Obviously, suitable precautions must be taken since these are both flammable and give off strong headache-producing fumes when heated.

Complete immersion in all three of these cleaning agents is also possible if you judge it worth the risk of disturbing any inks on the surface. Here again, past experience is important, but by touching some unimportant quarter of an inch of the inked area with each of the solvents—and keeping it wet for half an hour—you can determine what is reasonable safety or otherwise.

Stains

For old black stains, there is absolutely nothing that can be done, because they were made by ink having soot or some other source of carbon in them, and nothing in our universe is more stable.

For brown stains that look like the result of the paper's having gotten wet, proceed in the same way as in the instructions for *Mildew*, above. But the bleach to try first is the dilute solution of oxalic acid, because if what you have are truly simple water stains, it will certainly work. Rust, however, is as unmovable as carbon.

Mending

Aside from carefully gluing a tear back together with white glue—because it dries clear and remains pliable when used this way—there isn't much to be done about old paper that is falling apart. All you can do is to stop the process by spraying it with thymol (a form of formaldehyde) and, after it dries, pressing it between two pieces of glass.

For sealing the edges, plastic tapes look good and are easy to apply, but they won't last for more than a few years. Nor will the rubber cements last, not even the strong ones used for veneers. The best thing to do is to cut strips of paper three-quarters of an inch wide and apply epoxy glue to one side with your fingertip. Stick these on, and when the glue has set apply another coat to the outside of the paper.

PAPERWEIGHTS

See GLASSWARE.

PAPIER-MÂCHÉ

There are two kinds of papier-mâché. The older kind dates back to the early 1700s and was made by completely mashing —and even boiling—old paper to the consistency of mashed potatoes. This was then pressed into greased molds and allowed to dry. The resulting curved panels and moldings were glued onto boxes and the sides of cabinets, where they were japanned and decorated with oil paintings in the spare Japanese manner. Sometimes regular oil paintings typical of the period were also made on them.

The other way of making papier-mâché is to paste one layer of paper onto another with flour paste until it all becomes a soggy mat that can be molded into any shape you please. This became one of the wildly popular homecrafts of the Victorian era, and in extreme cases furniture was even made out of it, with or without supporting wooden frames.

The stuff can be mended with white glue, which the paper will suck in and which has the correct degree of pliability for the purpose. Once the piece is stabilized by the glue, cracks can be filled with black shellac sticks or black wax. (See also JAPANNING.)

PARCHMENT

Parchment is nothing more than the untanned skin of a sheep, goat, or calf that has been dried in the sun and sanded smooth on one or both sides. Chalk and/or lime may have been worked into it, and it can be very ancient—some pieces found in very dry caves going back as far as Old Testament times.

As the British say, it is a very liable material—meaning that it is very liable to change in some way for the worse if you do anything to it. About all that is ever essayed is to flatten out pieces that are folded or rolled and have become very hard and brittle.

This is done in a box or room that can be kept at high humidity—say, 85 per cent—but below condensation point. After twenty-four hours in such an environment, the straightening process is begun with wedges and small weights —*very* gradually. Movement of half an inch a day is all that should be forced. In other words, you have to think in terms of weeks or even months.

Parchment must be unrolled very slowly.

If any cleaning at all is to be tried, the best thing is unleaded gasoline, which is effective on the wax and grease stains that are common.

The trouble with parchment is, of course, that it has not been tanned—chemically treated to make its fibers pliable. In British, that's pliable as opposed to liable, of course. For contrast—if little help—see LEATHER.

PASTELS

A pastel is a drawing made on paper with colored chalk of varying degrees of greasiness. The earlier the pastel, generally speaking, the less grease and the more liability. In fact, downright friability, which in British means just about to fall apart.

The basic problem with pastels is that the chalk simply falls off the paper. You don't even have to breathe in the same room with it. And you can't spray it with lacquer because, while this will glue the chalk particles to the paper, it will also change their color. From a strict museum conservator's point of view, all you can do is to lay it on its back in an airtight display case made of heavy metal and bolted to a stone floor.

Come to think of it, that *is* about all anyone can do to preserve an old pastel. There is nothing at all positive that can be done. For once, I can only be completely defensive.

PEWTER

An alloy of lead and tin, pewterware is, in effect, cast solder, which is a metal that melts at low temperatures and is used for "gluing" together metals that melt at higher temperatures. (See JEWELRY.)

Being soft, pewter is easily polished with any silver polish or other fine abrasives such as jewelers' rouges. Collectors consider this an artistic sacrilege, but why the patina that pewter quickly acquires is so highly appreciated is somewhat of a mystery, for pewter's patina is a dead, dull, dark gray of no charm whatsoever. (Polished and lacquered to prevent tarnishing, it looks like a dark silver.)

If an old piece is found in a badly corroded state, it is usually best to grind and file it smooth, polish it with emery paper, and finally buff it with jewelers' buffing compounds and an electrically driven buffing wheel. (For more about this and everything else in this article, refer to JEWELRY.) However, you can also use acid to eat into the pewter and give it a violent cleaning job. For this you can use straight or diluted muriatic acid—which is already-diluted hydrochloric acid. The muriatic is sold in paint and hardware stores.

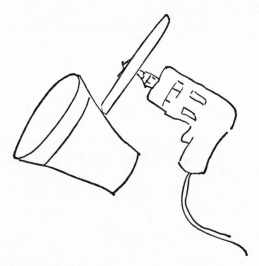

It is best to file, grind, sand, and buff corrosion off soft pewter.

Bending pewter back into shape is not hard, and it can be made easier if you warm it up in your oven to 350° F. and then plunge it into cold water two or three times to soften it further. Then you pound it back to shape with a soft padded hammer against a piece of wood you have carved into the shape at which you want the metal to stop bending. To make a padded hammer, you just tape about half an inch of felt over the pounding head of an ordinary hammer or heavy wooden mallet.

Now, as to soldering broken pewter—as in a cracked cup or spout or a broken-off handle or foot—there is no question that it can be done. But this takes us down a pathway so directly headed for disaster that I hesitate to go even a few steps with you.

To begin with, pewter can have varying amounts of copper and other metal in it that cause all kinds of variations in its melting point. The fellow down the street that successfully soldered his pewter may have been working with pewter having a melting point of 800° F., and yours may be only 400°. And he may have had a solder with a very low melting point, and yours may be high.

Therefore, you are really going to have to get into soldering by buying a soldering iron with a temperature control and special solder of the lowest melting temperature. In that event, such irons and solder are available from the Grieger's catalogue (see JEWELRY).

Pewter can be quite effectively mended with epoxy glue, however, if the surfaces to be joined are finely scored with a needle point first. For all work with epoxy glue see CERAMICS.

PHOTOGRAPHS

In the early 1900s along came Mr. Eastman and photography as we know it today: a positive print made on a light-sensitive emulsion based on paper. This print was made from a negative consisting of another light-sensitive emulsion on a clear plastic base. The improvement over previous methods was that any number of prints could be made from the negative.

Many negatives also were made on a glass base for larger professional cameras, with the same emulsion that was used on the plastic roll film. In both cases, if the old negative emulsion has faded or become hazed over, it can be vastly improved by redevelopment in an "intensifier."

You do not need a dark room to do this—just three small developing trays, or the equivalent, and running water in a kitchen sink. You put the plate—old film is rarely found—in the intensifier solution mixed according to the directions on the bottle and leave it for as long as the directions say. Then take it out and rinse it, in water under the faucet and put it into another tray full of "fixer" solution for twenty minutes, agitating it every two or three minutes. Then you wash it in a tray through which running water is slowly moving for a good two hours to be sure of removing the fixer. Water must not be above 70° F.—the emulsion will be ruined—or below 55° to be effective. Prints or enlargements are then made in the usual way.

Now, this is not a book on the chemistry of photography, and so I would at this point like to refer you to the Eastman Kodak Company's many authoritative reference booklets that are available through any photographic shop. The one to start with for intensifiers is found in their Professional Data Book series and is entitled *Processing Chemicals and Formulas*, price $1.00.

Paper prints cannot be restored or intensified chemically, but wonders can be done by rephotographing them with fine-grain film through various filters to eliminate brownish blotches. The negatives then can be printed on high-contrast paper to get stronger blacks and whites.

Of course, this is not actual restoration of the original print, but it is reclamation of the image that was once on it.

For old prints that have curled, photographic-supply stores sell a flattening agent that you add to water to make a bath in which to soak the prints. This works much better than soaking them in plain water. You can also dry prints by weighting them down between large white blotters that are also available through photographic-supply stores. In doing this, don't put the prints between the blotters dripping wet. First wipe them dry with paper towels and let them lie face down on a table for ten or fifteen minutes. Then start with the blotters, changing them as they dampen.

PORCELAIN

See CERAMICS.

RADIOS

There will be no discussion about whether a 1911 Atwater Kent radio is an antique or not. I have one, and if you don't think it is an antique, you are just jealous—as well you should be.

Nonsense aside, there is something very interesting about old radios that is not widely known. That is that they are quite easily repaired when they stop working, for there are only two parts in them that can wear out, and both are replaceable by anyone who can solder. (See JEWELRY.)

The first of these two parts is one of the old giant tubes. Most likely the burned-out one will be the one that doesn't heat up. At any rate, your local radio repair person will be able to test them all for you if you bring them in to him. Spray the sockets with Liquid Wrench to loosen their pins before removal.

Now, you won't be able to find a good big old tube to replace yours, but your radio repair person will be able to give you a new little one that performs the same function. He—or you—can also remove the old socket and wire in a new one that the new tube fits. Or the new little tube socket can be placed right on top of the old one.

The other thing that can wear out is a condenser, which is a "jelly roll" of paper and two sheets of tin foil that has been dipped in shellac. It is usually about three or four inches long and has wires from the two sheets of tin foil coming out each end. What has gone wrong with it is that the two sheets of tin foil are now touching. Modern versions of these devices are also available from your local radio repair person. Bring him the old one, and he will give you the modern equivalent. Smaller, but with the wires sticking out each end.

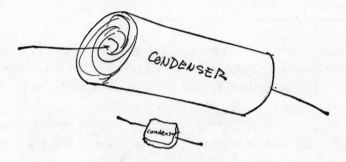

Old and new condensers.

The reason for not just taking the set to the repair man is that it is so big and heavy for you to move, and he doesn't want it taking up space in his usually tiny shop anyway. One way to avoid this is to take him the small schematic drawing of the way your set is connected up that was always pasted on the back or inside of these sets. For instance, if the condenser you take him is unmarked, he will be able to tell its capacity from the diagram.

SCRIMSHAW

The heyday of the American whaling industry came right after the War of 1812 (in which we had to lick the British all over again) and lasted into the 1870s, when much cheaper oil from the bowels of the earth began coming on the market. So that dates scrimshaw pretty definitely, for it consists of whales' teeth that were engraved and carved by the sailors aboard the whaling ships. These voyages of ten lasted as long as three years, and that left the sailors with a lot of time on their hands.

The results of their efforts range from crude drawings to exquisite ones made by incising the surface of the teeth and rubbing soot into the lines—not to mention many practical objects such as pie-edge crimpers for wives and sweethearts left at home. The engravings show old ships, harbors, scenery, and especially the business of whaling: whales blowing and the accidents that occurred when the whales were harpooned from longboats that were sent out from the mother ship. Of the most interesting of these, the forgeries are legion. After all, whales' teeth are ivory and as such are easy to carve and engrave. Nor is it hard to stain new teeth so that they look old by soaking them in strong tea or a stain made by boiling up a few wads of chewing tobacco. (They still sell as much chewing tobacco in shipbuilding places like Camden, Maine, as they ever did.) Snuff, too makes a good stain. ("Chaw" and snuff aren't fire hazards in yards that build wooden boats.)

For more about the techniques used to clean and restore scrimshaw, see IVORY.

SHIP MODELS

The commonest problem with old ship models is wilted rigging, and the first thing you do is to give it a good cleaning with a patented dry-cleaning fluid. Hold the boat sideways over a pan to catch your drippings and apply the cleaner with a camel's-hair brush.

It often is possible to shrink the old threads by repeatedly wetting them and putting them in the hot sun inside a window to dry out. Some will draw tight when brushed with a solution of 50 per cent shellac and 50 per cent denatured alcohol. Also, by cutting a tiny wedge in the flat end of a toothpick, you can roll up the slack into a tiny ball, which you glue down at the end of the thread where it will be least obtrusive. You glue it with about a fifth of a drop of model airplane cement, which dries very quickly. Then by sizing the thread with shellac or sprayed lacquer, you can prevent future sagging.

If the sails need restoration, see TEXTILES and DOLLS (for dolls' clothes, of course).

For cleaning decks and hulls, a good brushing with artists' bristle brushes of the kind used in oil painting comes first. Then use the dry-cleaning fluid again because it won't soften any glue or dissolve any paint—which is important, since water colors were often used.

For retouching the lovely muted and faded colors, you can get perfect matches if you find an art-supply store that carries the Winsor and Newton line of designer's *gouache*. These also dry to the dull texture usually desired, but they can be glossed by coating them with shellac or lacquer.

Incidentally, colors are not muted to match faded old paints by adding gray or black to them, but by adding just a smidgen of the color that is opposite on a color wheel. Just a touch of burnt sienna in any blue works well, ultramarine in the reddish and brown shades.

The best solution to the sagging-rigging problem that I have ever seen was on a fantastically perfect model of a whaling ship made by an old man in Nantucket about fifty years ago. He used fine silk-covered copper wire from a coil found in an old radio, and that wire hasn't wilted yet. Of course, that might be because he also did the best thing you can do to preserve any ship model. He put it in an airtight glass case —an upside-down tropical fish aquarium.

SILVER PLATE

See GOLD PLATE, JEWELRY, and SILVERWARE.

SILVERWARE

Silver has been used for eating utensils, cups, bowls, and so forth since ancient times, but those are all in museums, or should be. The silverware we get to see is English and American, starting around the time of Queen Anne, and it divides into five classes of "product": fine or pure silver, Sheffield, sterling, electroplate on copper, and electroplate on "German" silver.

Fine (pure or almost pure) silver is almost as soft, malleable, and ductile as pure gold and doesn't corrode in normal environments. It especially doesn't rust. While it will certainly tarnish, it doesn't combine with elements in foods to make poisons the way copper will. (Which is why copper is used only for boiling water and why copper frying pans used in many French restaurants are silver-plated on the inside.)

From the early 1700s we have some beautifully designed forks made of silver so soft that the tines bend when you try to stick them into a steak. And bowls and cups that will bend in your fingers.

It was soon discovered that when a small amount of copper was added to the silver it could be hardened a lot. This was important to its use in coins—as in the British pound sterling, which consists by law of 925 parts of silver and 75 parts of copper. So this standard was adopted for all British-made silverware that could be stamped "Sterling." It is the basic silver of England and the American colonies—as represented by Paul Revere and many other fine American silversmiths. (It is still the standard for modern silverware in utensils and art objects.)

The next innovation in the use of silver came around the middle of the eighteenth century when someone got the idea of rolling thin sheets of silver onto one or both sides of a sheet of copper, with heat and pressure applied to make the two metals fuse. The sheets were then shaped by hammering them on forms, mostly into bowls. This was called Sheffield plate, and its manufacture went on for about a hundred years until supplanted by the electroplating process around the middle of the nineteenth century.

In electroplating, an object is manufactured in copper. Then the object and a piece of silver are both suspended in a mild cyanide solution and an electric current is passed from the silver to the copper. This causes molecules of the silver to pass through the solution and to be deposited on the copper. Only a thin layer of the silver can be deposited before the action stops. But if you remove the object being plated, clean the silver coating, and put it back into the solution, another layer of silver will be deposited. Thus, we have double, triple, and quadruple plate. (If you first cover the surface of baby shoes with graphite, you can electroplate them, too, the same way.)

You obviously can tell if an object is sterling silver or plated by cutting into it with a triangular file to see if there is copper beneath the surface. This is regularly done on the bottoms of bowls and in other unobtrusive places, so much so that the value of a piece so tested is not considered to diminish. After all, it was the English who originated the idea that it is not enough for justice to be done—justice must be seen to have been done.

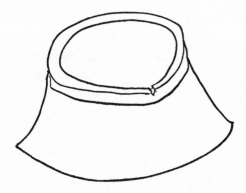

Test for silver with file cut.

We finally come to the nefarious practice of using the electroplating process to put a silver coating on "German" silver. German silver is not silver at all, but an imitation of silver made by mixing nickel and zinc with copper. The proportions are about two-thirds copper, one-third nickel, and a dash of zinc. There was no exact standard. The trouble is that since it looks just like silver, it is hard to detect even with a file cut made in the base of such an object. The German silver objects that were not plated even tarnish the same way silver does.

However, there is a chemical test for real silver that is easily performed with nitric acid. This is not the 5 per cent solution that drugstores sell, but the full-strength kind that eats into almost anything except the bottle it comes in. You have to get it from a chemical-supply house, which you find by asking your local jeweler. At any rate, when a drop of nitric acid is put on pure silver, it foams up pure white. On sterling silver it foams cream-colored. On copper and German silver it turns green.

Cleaning of silver is done with fine abrasives from pumice down to jeweler's rouge; these are ingredients in all the patented paste cleaners. For cleaning pieces with deep crevices, the various dips on the market are perfectly safe. Professional cleaning services clean silver by first reversing the electroplating process and then reapplying another coat of silver to replace any lost in the reverse process.

If you want to correct bending or dents in sterling silver—or even plated copper—the work is made much easier if you first anneal the piece by bringing it up to 1100° F. and quenching it in water. Obviously, this requires a special oven of the kind used for enameling copper and is sold in advanced hobby shops. An experienced silversmith can teach you how to do it with a blowtorch.

For soldering silver and lots of other interesting information see JEWELRY.

STAINED GLASS

There are two kinds of stained glass. The first is the kind used in the windows of buildings, such as the cathedral at Chartres, in which enclosed space I defy any man to stand and not *know* that he has an immortal soul. In these windows the pieces of colored glass are held in place by cames, which are H-shaped strips of soft lead, with the edge of one glass piece entering one compartment of the H and the edge of the adjoining glass piece entering the other compartment. The lead is then pressed tight, and the ends of the pieces of came are soldered together. The work is done on a large flat table, and sections of it are mounted in metal or wooden frames—which are then assembled in the window space.

In the olden days—like around A.D. 1300—these lead cames were cast and drawn, and there is nothing to stop you from doing the same thing if you get deeply involved in this sort of work. However, you can buy a number of sizes of cames from a company called Whittmore-Durgin—see address below—which will also supply you with pieces of glass. If you prefer to call in outside help, the architect responsible for the most recently built church in your area will be able to tell you the name of the nearest company practicing this craft or art. They have long ladders and will travel.

The second kind of stained-glass work is the kind found in the so-called Tiffany-type lamp shades. It is also found in real Tiffany lamp shades, but I am diffident about telling you how to work on anything worth from $2,500 to $30,000. However, Tiffany's work was widely imitated for the mass market, and

it is in the restoration of such pieces that we are mostly interested.

So this is the way the shades are made—with the implica-
tions for restoration or imitation being obvious.

You begin with a wooden form in the shape of the shade to
be made. Forms made of Styrofoam can now be bought in
many sizes and shapes. Cover the form with a paper pattern
on which you draw the design you wish to make with the
pieces of glass. You then take the pattern off and lay it on a
flat table. Then place a piece of colored glass on the pattern
and trace one of the shapes onto it with a grease pencil. With
a glass cutter and glass-trimming pliers you cut your glass
roughly to shape, and finish-trim it on a grindstone.

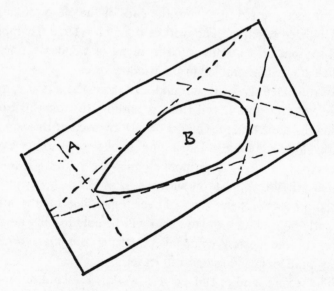

(A) *is original sheet of glass.* (B) *is finally
desired shape, which has been traced on glass
with grease pencil. Dotted lines are preliminary straight-line cuts.*

Now, if this sounds hard to do, you are absolutely right. However, there is a method that will help. First, you cut the glass in a rectangle or rhomboid just a little bit larger than your shape. Cutting a straight line along the edge of a wooden ruler is easy if you have a new glass cutter and never go back over a cut once it is made (recutting will immediately ruin the edge of your glass cutter).

Your curved cuts may now be made freehand after lots of practice or by guiding the cutter against a preshaped wooden edge. You can make yourself a set of curved templates out of masonite, cutting it with a band saw or saber saw.

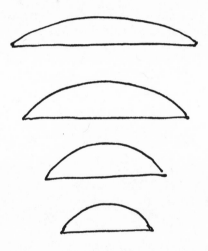

Templates with different degrees of curve can be used to guide glass cutter.

The final step is to grind off the excess glass with a grindstone, supporting the piece of glass with a piece of wood as you push it against the stone.

Now you take a strip of copper three-eighths of an inch wide (wider for thicker glass) and press it around the edge of

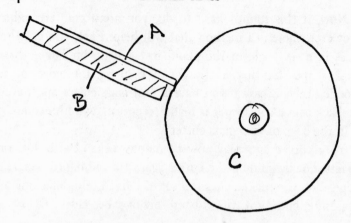

*Rough edges are trimmed off the glass (A)
with a grindstone (C) while glass is supported
by a block of wood (B) to prevent cracking.*

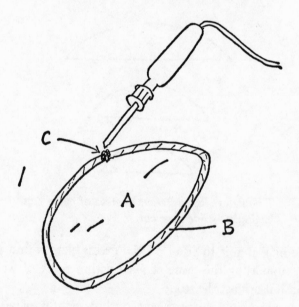

*After the glass (A) has been edged by having
a thin strip of copper (B) bent around it, the
ends of the strip are soldered together.*

your shaped piece of glass. Where the ends meet, you solder the copper together. Then, after you have cut and copper-edged all your pieces of glass, you assemble them on your form and solder all the copper edges together. Just look at a shade carefully, and all this will be perfectly clear.

That is the process, and since it and the materials used are so basic it is possible, if one wishes to take the pains, to reproduce *exactly* the original antique product of Victorian times. With the current interest in fine Victoriana, this is being done by a lot of crafty old forgers in secret back rooms of antique shops and interior-decorator places. While the job is time consuming, they are getting well paid. As this is written, they are getting around $250 to the trade for the kind of shade that hung over Victorian dining-room tables—retail price, $350 plus.

In the interest of clarity, I have left out a number of details in the description of the basic process. So here they are, in what I consider their logical place and order.

The Glass

The best glass for repairs is obtained by cannibalizing badly smashed pieces of the same kind. This can be obtained not only from shades but also from stained-glass windows used in churches and houses during the late-Victorian era. Also, stained glass is still being made in many colors, because there is a continuing market for it in the construction of new churches and mausoleums. Not to mention Tiffany lampshade forgers.

Of course, it is hard to specify a color of glass in words, but if you can send a sample piece there is a mail-order house that is devoted exclusively to finding and selling stained glass and other supplies to anyone interested. "No order too large or too small." Send $.50 for their catalogue. The name of these "stained-glass persons," as they call themselves, is Whittmore-Durgin, Hanover, Massachusetts 02339. They also have a large store in Hanover where you can make your own selections.

The Copper

Obviously, you need copper of the same thickness as the object you are repairing. Your source for this is either your plumber or the local supply house that he uses. Real craftsmen that they are, plumbers are always interested in things like this and are glad to help you out.

Copper can also be obtained from lumberyards, and the standard thickness used for flashing windows happens to be the right thickness for most jobs. All this copper has been considerably hardened by rolling, and unless it happens to be a very soft batch, you will want to anneal it by heating it with a blowtorch until it begins to glow red, and then plunging it into water. After cleaning it with steel wool, you will then be able to cut it very easily with metal-cutting shears. The width of your strips is determined by unsoldering and flattening one of those originally used. Whittmore-Durgin also sells rolls of copper stripping in the widths most commonly used.

A strip is now bent around the edge of each piece of glass to be used, and the ends of the strip are soldered together. The copper-edged pieces of glass are then assembled on the mold. The original molds were wood, but you can shape yours from a block of plastic foam or make one out of papier-mâché. You need only to make a soggy mat with ten or twelve layers of newspaper glued together with flour paste, press it inside the shade to get the shape, and then let it dry. You can even let it dry inside the shade if you use a layer of wax paper or aluminum foil to keep it from sticking.

Soldering

Ordinary resin-core solder is fine, and the easiest to use. But do get a small soldering iron from your local craft and hobby shop. And before proceeding, read JEWELRY, which tells a lot about soldering.

Antiquing

The final step is to darken the new copper, and you start by removing all traces of solder or anything else from it—such as the barely visible tarnish that will start to form on it in a few hours. Steel wool is not very good for this, as it doesn't get into cracks and crevices. The best thing to use is kitchen cleansing powder, which you rub in hard with a stiff toothbrush. Rinse well, and then scrub with powdered pumice and water. Then rinse while scrubbing with the toothbrush, and dry with paper towels. Immediately apply the 5 per cent solution of nitric acid available through your local pharmacy. This will turn the copper a brown that matches the patina on the rest of the copper. If it isn't dark enough, additional applications after drying and warming the copper will do the job.

TEXTILES

Fine old woven fabrics—from Persian rugs to pink silk ribbons—should only be dry cleaned—and then only after an unobtrusive area of the fabric has been tested.

For really delicate materials, lay them on a screen over a pan, sprinkle the cleaning fluid on them with a small watering can or a spray, and just let it drain through the fabric. The best cleaner to use is carbon tetrachloride, which is available from paint and hardware stores. Its odor soon fades, and it leaves no oily residue. It is also nonflammable, and the fumes aren't too strong, though good ventilation will keep you from getting a headache.

Vacuum cleaning of delicate fabrics can also be tried. It will be made much safer if you mount the fabric between two screens to keep it from sucking up into the nozzle.

In any event, water should never be used on anything valuable. You often hear that the old vegetable dyes are stable. But this is not always true; it may have been true up to recently but is no longer so in any given piece. The vegetable dyes probably got their undeserved reputation because they *are* so much better than the aniline dyes the Germans introduced in the late 1800s. But the comparison doesn't mean much when you consider how fugitive the early aniline dyes were—and how fugitive the current ones still are. The worst part of that story is that within a few years of their introduction they were being used all over the world, because they were so cheap. That means that they were used in some Persian rugs almost a hundred years ago. In spite of strong government concern they are still sometimes used. *Caveat emptor.*

Truly fragile pieces of great historical value should be sprayed on both sides with lacquer, which by permeating and surrounding the fibers gives them a new structure that will hold them together indefinitely if the piece is not handled and is kept in an airtight glass case.

Mildew is best prevented and treated with thymol, a derivative of formaldehyde, which is a pharmaceutical supply, although your druggist will have to order it specially for you. For more about this and some related problems, see PAPER.

If a piece of fabric is to be hung for display—as is often done with old flags—it should first be sewn onto a sheet of felt or sailcloth, and that in turn, is hung from sewn-on loops. Even hung like this, fabrics may still be attacked by moths, and so for permanent protection they should be hung in more-or-less airtight cases, with mothballs added once a year. Incidentally, even rugs lying on the floor will be attacked by moths in a house that is left empty for more than a year.

TINTYPES

Just before and during the Civil War the daguerreotype was supplanted by a cheaper and sturdier single-image photograph called the tintype. In this case the light-sensitive chemicals were laid on a piece of black-enameled tin.

These do not fade or tarnish like daguerreotypes, but the emulsion surface is usually unprotected, and so they get scratched, dented, and just plain dirty.

Mild soap and water will clean them, but don't scrub hard or use any abrasive. Soap and water will usually work wonders in improving their brightness, but it will also make any scratches or chips caused by bending look worse.

Such physical abuse can be made unnoticeable to a remarkable degree if you get from a photographic-supply house (ask your local photographer) a set of professional retouching paints. These contain a number of shades of grays and browns that are perfect for the work. Since they are water colors, they are easily wiped off if you don't like your first tries.

After retouching, you can give the surface a protective coating with a spray can of clear lacquer. Dull or matte lacquer looks the most authentic.

WATCHES AND CLOCKS

If the mechanism of a clock or watch has been broken or even just worn out, it would be pure fantasy to suggest that you could learn to repair it from a book—even a whole book or ten books. A bearing hole that has worn to the point where it is loose has to be drilled larger and have a new bearing, or bushing, fixed into the hole. Worn or damaged gears are not repaired but replaced. They have to be cut from sheets of brass and new teeth filed into the edges. Even your local watchmaker doesn't have either the machinery or skills to do this. He has to send the part to a factory that specializes in this kind of work.

However, it also happens to be true that more than 90 per cent of all watches and clocks that won't run are not physically damaged or worn at all but merely dirty. It does not take any special skill or machinery to get them going again by cleaning and reoiling them. As with all restoration, though, the matter must be approached in a calm frame of mind and executed carefully and patiently.

Obviously, it is easier to work with a clock than with a watch because it is larger. You can see everything without a magnifying glass. The only real difference is that for cleaning a watch you will have to buy a set of watchmaker's screw drivers and a jeweler's loupe. (If they are not available locally, order them from the mail-order catalogue of the Brookstone Company, Peterborough, New Hampshire 03458.) For the purpose of getting at and cleaning them, the construction of *old* watches and clocks is the same.

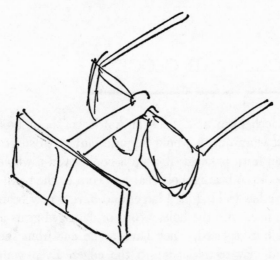

Flip-up magnifiers that clip to any eye glasses.
(Brookstone Catalogue)

The first step is to remove the face of your clock or watch so you can take off the hands by gently prying with your screw driver. *Do not* use needle-nosed pliers, for these will bend the hands. If they do not come off easily, apply a drop of Liquid Wrench, and let it work overnight.

Now, go around to the back of your clock or watch, and with some thoughtful inspection you will soon discover the screws that remove the works intact so that you can get at them from both sides.

The cleaning is then done with benzene—from your pharmacy—and fine brushes. Never touch the brass gears with anything except a toothpick—in the case of a watch, a thin, sharpened toothpick. A few days of soaking in the benzene may be needed after the initial brush cleaning. Then brush again. Gasoline or lighter fluid or Liquid Wrench can be used for the preliminary soakings and brushings, as long as the last liquid used is pure, clean benzene. If you get really interested in this, you can buy or make a wire basket that you vibrate while it holds a watch in the benzene. A couple of hours of shaking is the equivalent of many overnight soakings and daily brushings.

In the case of a clock mechanism that is very dirty and has layers of dust-laden oil all over the gears, you can—after a first brushing with gasoline—simmer it for four or five hours in a gallon of water to which you have added a cup or two of ammonia: just ammonia, nothing else—and not the sudsy kind, either. You can also reach in with a wooden spoon and jiggle the works every once in a while. Then remove the works from the ammonia water and place it in plain boiling water, which you allow to cool slowly. Finally, rinse under cold running water. Then, before the works dry, rinse them by pouring denatured alcohol over them to suck any water out of the bearings, and blow them dry. Then clean with benzene as above.

Now for the secret of oiling. You buy some watch and clock oil from your local jeweler, and apply *small* drops of it to the bearings only, using a dry camel's-hair brush to suck up any excess that hasn't been sucked into the bearing. You *do not* oil any of the gears, large or small. Instead, on a clock use a pointed camel's-hair brush to just touch them with pow-

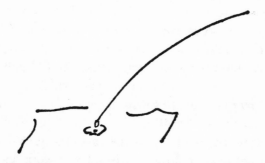

Use thin wire to get small drops of oil for bearing.

dered graphite. On a watch, you touch them with a camel's-hair brush that you have rubbed on a piece of billiard chalk.

Finally, you cannot get some old watches to go without oiling the escapement gear points. In such a case, they are going to have to be cleaned and reoiled periodically—every time the watch stops. The alternative, of course, would be a very expensive rebuilding.

Grandfather Clocks

Whenever I have seen a long-pendulum clock that didn't work, I have been told that the reason was either (1) "We can't seem to get it level" or (2) "Something is broken it it." Well, in 99 per cent of the cases (pun intended) nothing is broken.

The trouble almost invariably turns out to be that the works are "dirty." This means that enough dust has gotten into the oil in the bearings to turn it into a gum. Or, even worse, that some misguided soul has at some time put oil on the teeth of the gears, and these have gummed up. It is not that the lubricating oil itself thickens, as many people seem to think. A lubricating oil is a mineral oil, and its consistency is stable, like that of any other mineral. The problem is always the dust.

Obviously, then, the way to keep the dust out is to seal the back of the case. Also, when you are restoring one of these old clocks, you should apply a coat of shellac to the inside of the case. This prevents the creation of dust by the pulverization of the surface of ancient dry wood, which is constantly "shaken" by the action of the mechanism.

As to cleaning such works, it is possible to do the job without removing the works from the case—the preferred course of action not only because it saves a lot of work but also because it eliminates the danger of damaging the release mechanism.

The first step, of course, is to dust and seal the inside of the case. Use shellac and a brush rather than a spray can to avoid having the dust of the sprayed shellac or lacquer make matters even worse in your works.

Then you wash the works with Liquid Wrench, which shoots out of a pressure can in a thin stream. This stuff is called a "penetrating solvent," and it sure is. For a substitute you could use gasoline with a little lubricating oil (5 per cent) mixed into it, applying it with a camel's-hair brush.

Give the works about three rinses with this solvent about an hour apart, moving the works after each application by gently pushing the pendulum to get things in motion. This will get your works going again—barring that rare case of actual damage—but then the solvent must be flushed off the gears with benzene—or lighter fluid or rubber-cement solvent, which are the same thing. This can be brushed or sprayed on with a baby air-brush device now being sold in most hardware stores; this is good for the purpose if not much good for spraying anything thicker.

Finally, oil the bearings, using a fine camel's-hair brush to apply as little oil as possible. What you use is a thin lubricating oil usually called "clock and watch oil," obtainable most easily from your local watchmaker.

WATER COLORS

Cleaning water colors is impossible, and even looking at them in a bright light is destructive to them. As for preservation, they can be impregnated with thymol from behind and sealed between two pieces of glass before framing and hanging (see PASTELS).

INDEX

Acetic acid, for copper, 47
Acetone, for marble, 131
Acids (*see also* specific acids):
  for bronze patina, 13; for
  copper patina, 47; and
  etchings, 56; and marble, 131
Adam furniture, 63
Airbrushes, 24–25, 39, 195
Alabaster, 1–2
Alcohol: for ceramics, 28; for
  daguerreotypes, 50; to dissolve
  phonograph records, 17; for
  furniture finishing, 65, 66,
  68ff.; for lithograph solution,
  124–25; for marble, 131; for oil
  paintings, 146, 147, 149, 157,
  158; for ship models, 176;
  storing brushes in, 17; as
  thinner (*see* specific
  substances); for watches,
  clocks, 193
Amber, 3
American Dynasty, 115
Ammonia: for bottles, 10; for
  brass, 12; for ceramics, 27; in
  glass cleaning, 82; for
  limestone, 122; for marble,
  132; in resilvering mirrors, 140,
  141; for watches or clocks, 193
Ammonium chloride, 47–48, 117
Aneroid barometer, 4–6
Aniline dyes, 69, 188
Animal hides and hooves (*see
  also* Parchment): glue of, 28,
  78; for sizing (*see* Paper)
Annealing, 45, 46, 180, 186;
  locks, 128
Antique Trader, The, 57–58
Asphaltum, 106–8

Atlas Master Mending Kit,
  36–37, 85
Atlas Minerals & Chemicals, 37

Baby shoes, silver-plating, 179
Ball bearings, to polish bottles,
  11
Barometers, 4–6
Battery acid, for bronze, 13, 14
Beeswax: for doll repair, 52–53;
  for ivory, 103, 104, 105; for
  leather, 9, 118, 119; for
  limestone, 122; for marble,
  139; and oil paintings, 144,
  150ff.
Bentwood furniture, 58
Benzene: for alabaster, 1; for
  aneroid barometers, 5; for cloth
  bindings, 8; for leather, 9, 118;
  for marble, 131, 133; and
  paper stains, 164; for watches
  or clocks, 192, 193
Bindings, book, 7–9
Biscuit, 43
Biscuit porcelain, 42
Bisque, 43; dolls, 52
"Bloom," on oil paintings,
  157–58
Blotters: for curled photos, 172;
  for stained paper, 164
Bluing, for locks, 128
"Blush," 19
Bone ash, in china, 42
Bone china, 42
Book lice, 6–7
Books, 6–10. *See also* Paper
Bottles, 10–11
Bowling-alley wax, for marble,
  135

Spouts: reattaching, 30, 33;
replacing, 36
Staffordshire ceramics, 42
Stained glass, 181–87; antiquing,
187; forgeries, 57; obtaining
the copper, 186; obtaining the
glass, 185–86; soldering copper,
185, 187
Stainless steel, and gold plate, 91
Stains (see also Patinas; specific
bleaches): in alabaster, 2; in
bottles, 11; for furniture,
69–70, 78; in glass, 83; for
gunstock, 102; in leather, 119;
in marble, 132–34; in paper,
159, 164–65; for scrimshaw,
175
Stalactites and stalagmites, 1
Statues. See Limestone; Marble
Statuettes, repairing ceramic,
36
Steaming dents in gunstock, 99
Steel: and gold plate, 91;
soldering, 108
Steel wool: and "blush," 19; on
bronze, 13; on bronze powder
decoration, 20; and furniture
finishing, 66, 67, 68, 71, 73,
75, 77; and gun cleaning,
finishing, 96, 101, 102; and
japanning, 107
Stencils, for bronze powder
decoration, 15–16, 17–19
Sterling silver, 177
Stick barometer, 4, 5
Stone carving. See specific stones
Sunshine, 27, 132

Table legs, regluing, 79
Table tops (see also Marble):
distressing, 78
Tarnish. See specific metals
Tea, to stain scrimshaw, 175
Textiles, 188–89 (see also Cloth
bindings); dolls' clothing,
50–51

Thiourea, and daguerreotypes, 50
Thymol: for books, 6–7, 8, 10;
for oil paintings on wood, 158;
for paper, 162–63, 165; for
textiles, 189; for water colors,
195
Tiffany-type lamp shades, 181–87
Tin (see also Pewter; Solder and
soldering; Tintypes): bronze
powder decoration, 15; foil, in
condensers, 173; gold leaf on,
90; japanned trays, 107
Tintypes, 189–90
TM-4, 68
Tobacco stain: for paper, 164; for
scrimshaw, 175
Toothpicks, for watches or
clocks, 192
Treasure Jewels, 39
Tri-sodium-phosphate (t.s.p.):
for copper, 47; for lead, 117;
for limestone, 122; and
oil-soaked gunstock, 101
Tubes, radio, 173
Turpentine: for japanning, 107;
in restoring oil paintings, 146,
147, 149, 154

Urns, lead, 117

Vacuum cleaning textiles, 188
Varnish: and bronze powder
decoration, 17, 18; and
furniture finish, 67, 68, 72–73;
in gold leafing, 88, 90; and
japanning, 107; on oil
paintings, 145ff., 157–58; and
steaming gunstock, 99
Vaseline, for leather, 9
Velvet; 18, 90
Verdigris, 45
Vinegar: for bottles, 10; for
brass, 12; and bronze patina,
14; for ceramics, 27; for copper
patina, 47; for glass cleaning,
82; for lead patina, 117; to